Diagnosing
Autism
Spectrum Disorders

D1104642

Donald P. Gallo

Diagnosing Autism
Spectrum Disorders
A Lifespan Perspective

⟨W⟩WILEY-BLACKWELL

A John Wiley & Sons, Ltd, Publication

This edition first published 2010
© 2010 Donald P. Gallo

Wiley-Blackwell is an imprint of John Wiley & Sons, formed by the merger of Wiley's global Scientific, Technical, and Medical business with Blackwell Publishing.

Registered Office
John Wiley & Sons Ltd, The Atrium, Southern Gate, Chichester, West Sussex, PO19 8SQ, UK

Editorial Offices
The Atrium, Southern Gate, Chichester, West Sussex, PO19 8SQ, UK
9600 Garsington Road, Oxford, OX4 2DQ, UK
350 Main Street, Malden, MA 02148-5020, USA

For details of our global editorial offices, for customer services, and for information about how to apply for permission to reuse the copyright material in this book please see our website at www.wiley.com/wiley-blackwell.

The right of the author to be identified as the author of the editorial material in this work has been asserted in accordance with the Copyright, Designs and Patents Act 1988.

All rights reserved. No part of this publication may be reproduced, stored in a retrieval system, or transmitted, in any form or by any means, electronic, mechanical, photocopying, recording or otherwise, except as permitted by the UK Copyright, Designs and Patents Act 1988, without the prior permission of the publisher.

Wiley also publishes its books in a variety of electronic formats. Some content that appears in print may not be available in electronic books.

Designations used by companies to distinguish their products are often claimed as trademarks. All brand names and product names used in this book are trade names, service marks, trademarks or registered trademarks of their respective owners. The publisher is not associated with any product or vendor mentioned in this book. This publication is designed to provide accurate and authoritative information in regard to the subject matter covered. It is sold on the understanding that the publisher is not engaged in rendering professional services. If professional advice or other expert assistance is required, the services of a competent professional should be sought.

Library of Congress Cataloging-in-Publication Data

Gallo, Donald P.
Diagnosing autism : a lifespan perspective / by Donald P. Gallo.
    p. cm.
Includes bibliographical references and index.
ISBN 978-0-470-74924-1 (cloth) – ISBN 978-0-470-74923-4 (pbk.)   1. Autism–Diagnosis.   I. Title.
[DNLM: 1. Autistic Disorder–diagnosis. WM 203.5 G172d 2009]
RC553.A88.G35 2009
616.85′882075–dc22

                                                                                            2009035846

A catalogue record for this book is available from the British Library.

Typeset in 11/13pt Minion by Aptara Inc., New Delhi, India.
Printed in Singapore by Markono Print Media Pte Ltd

1   2010

For my loving family. To Emily and Josh—I wish that all parents would be as blessed as I have been with such wonderful children. To Debbie—you are my everything.

Contents

Preface   ix

Acknowledgments   xiii

About the Author   xv

1. A Brief Look at the History of Autism   1

2. The Importance of the Autism Referral   5

3. How to Conduct the Evaluation   17

4. Information to Gather at the Outset of the Evaluation   33

5. Diagnostic Criteria for the Autism Spectrum Disorders   39

6. The Main Problem Areas of Autism: Social Impairment   45

7. The Main Problem Areas of Autism: Language Impairment   61

8. The Main Problem Areas of Autism: Behavioral Concerns   79

9. Additional Questions to be Asked when Interviewing Teens   87

10. Additional Questions to be Asked when Interviewing Adults   97

11. Other Important Factors to Take into Consideration   105

12. Differential Diagnosis through the Lifespan   117

13. Feedback for the Patient and Family/Parents   143

Appendix A: Sample Copy of My Questionnaire   151

Appendix B: Sample Copies of Reports   157

References   179

Index   181

Preface

In late 2000, I was hired by Kaiser-Permanente to be the psychologist for their Autism Spectrum Disorder Diagnostic Service in the San Fernando Valley of Los Angeles. This position came about because California's Assembly Bill 88 requires insurance plans to provide coverage for the diagnosis and medically necessary treatment of nine severe mental illnesses, including autism and pervasive developmental disorder.

Between my position there and my private practice, I have conducted approximately 1,500 evaluations on a wide variety of individuals ranging in age from 12 months to 65 years. I typically conduct five to six evaluations a week. In the beginning, I was seeing mostly young children for autism evaluations after receiving referrals from their pediatricians. After a while, I began seeing patients in all age ranges, from 16 months to 55 years old.

At first, I relied rather heavily on the use of formal screening devices, such as the Childhood Autism Rating Scale (CARS) and the Gilliam Autism Rating Scale (GARS), in addition to the wisdom of a senior psychologist who had worked with Dr. Ivar Lovaas at University of California at Los Angeles decades earlier. Dr. Lovaas is one of the early pioneers of applied behavioral analysis, a way of modifying the behavior of children with autism.

As time progressed and I conducted more evaluations, attended more conferences, and read more books about autism, I increased my understanding of the vastness of the autism spectrum and the need to broaden my approach to more fully comprehend and appropriately diagnose these individuals. In addition, the early childhood rating scales did not translate easily for adults. As you could imagine, it would be more difficult for the mother of a 40-year-old man to recall early developmental milestones than the mother of a four-year-old.

In 2001, I created my own screening questionnaire, which is reproduced in Appendix A. This questionnaire is not any type of empirically validated instrument but more of the questions that encompass all aspects of the spectrum that I feel are necessary to make an appropriate diagnosis. By the time I felt comfortable in my ability to appropriately identify children on the spectrum, I was beginning to see a broader array of ages and was reading other professionals' reports in which they and I appeared to have vastly different pictures of the same individual.

I was diagnosing children and teens as "being on the spectrum" after their parents reported a history consistent with the disorder, and my observations of the individual in my office were consistent with what the parents had told me. However, other professionals were coming up with alternative diagnoses. Children I diagnosed with autism were being diagnosed with ADHD, obsessive-compulsive disorder, and anxiety disorders, without autism being considered as the reason for the child's problems.

In an effort to better understand the reasons for these various diagnoses, I placed a few phone calls to other experienced autism professionals throughout the Los Angeles area, whose opinion I respected. When I spoke with Dr. Laurie Stephens, the former director of the Help Group Center for Autism Spectrum Disorders and now the Director of Clinical Services for Education Spectrum in Alta Dena, California, she reported that she too was facing the same difficulties that I was, namely, that the combination of the broadness of the autism spectrum, the high number of children and teens being evaluated, and the lack of a commensurate number of professionals trained to diagnose autism created a great deal of missed or incorrect diagnoses.

This was the main reason why I felt the need to write this book. I consider myself quite lucky to have been able to learn how to identify symptoms of the autism spectrum in an environment including other trained professionals who have had significant experience in that area and were trained by leaders in the field. What about the other professionals who do not have that opportunity or who are not exposed to individuals on the spectrum in the numbers that I have seen because of working for such a large organization? Conducting evaluations with children and teens who may have autism on an occasional, monthly, or fortnightly basis is incredibly different than seeing a half-dozen children and teens for evaluations every week for the past 10 years.

This book is formatted to follow the chronology of an autism evaluation from start to finish. In Chapter 1, a very brief synopsis of the history of autism is presented. While that topic could fill an entire book on its own, only the information that provides the reader with background information about autism and helps them to answer the main question posed by this book is included; namely, does the person you are evaluating have an autism spectrum disorder?

In Chapters 2 and 3, information that is necessary for the professional to consider before even seeing the child is presented. Chapter 4 focuses on additional questions that need to be asked before autism is even considered. Chapter 5 lists the diagnostic criteria of the autism spectrum disorders, while Chapters 6–8 delve into the specific areas of impairment that are necessary for a diagnosis of autism. Within each of those three chapters, information will be presented about several different ranges and the type of information that needs to be obtained before a diagnosis can be made or ruled out.

Chapter 9 consists of additional questions to ask when interviewing teens and their families, while Chapter 10 covers interviewing adults and the particular challenges inherent in doing so. Chapter 11 is a compilation of supplemental information that I have found to be extremely helpful in making a diagnosis but are not factors included in the *DSM-IV-TR*. Chapter 12 includes the numerous "rule-out diagnoses" that need to be considered before a diagnosis is finalized. The final chapter, Chapter 13, deals with the conclusion of the evaluation and ways to impart your findings to the patient and their parents or family. Copies of the questionnaire I created, as well as sample reports, are also included. Examples of evaluations I have conducted will also be presented throughout the book.

While this book is obviously not all that a professional would need to be qualified to conduct autism evaluations, it provides the reader with "real-world" experiences and examples that they would not receive, or potentially even think about, from learning about this disorder in a classroom.

Acknowledgments

I owe a great debt of gratitude to Kaiser-Permanente in general and Dr. Len Sushinsky in particular for having faith that a newly licensed psychologist can not only handle but also excel in the position that I was given. I would also like to thank Susan Bassett for her constant support and for being such a wonderful coworker. A special thanks to Dr. Jerrold Parrish for all of his editing assistance and brainstorming, not to mention all the wonderful coffee.

About the Author

Dr Donald P. Gallo was born and raised in Los Angeles, California. After graduating from California State University, Northridge with his bachelor's degree in Psychology, Dr Gallo attended Teachers College, Columbia University in New York City, where he earned his first Master's degree, in Developmental Psychology.

After leaving New York, Dr Gallo returned to California and attended the California School of Professional Psychology, where he earned his second Master's degree, as well as his Ph.D. in Clinical Child Psychology. In 2003, Dr Gallo became board certified in Clinical Psychology by the American Board of Professional Psychology.

Dr Gallo works for Kaiser-Permanente in the San Fernando Valley of Los Angeles as the psychologist for their Autism Spectrum Disorders Diagnostic Service. He also maintains a private practice in Woodland Hills, California, with his wife, Deborah, who is also a child psychologist.

Dr Gallo can be contacted through his websites, www.donaldgallo.com and www.thedoctorsgallo.com

Chapter 1

A Brief Look at the History of Autism

In 1910, the Swiss psychiatrist Eugen Bleuler, while talking about schizophrenia, a term that he coined, used the Latin word *autismus* as a way of describing some of the symptoms of the disorder. The word *autismus* is derived from the Greek word *autos*, which means "self"; the English translation of *autismus* is "autism".

Twenty years later, Leo Kanner, an Austrian-born physician, developed the first child psychiatry program at Johns Hopkins Hospital in Baltimore, Maryland. His first book, *Child Psychiatry*, came out in 1935 and was the first English-language textbook to focus on the mental health issues of children. In 1943, he wrote a paper entitled "Autistic Disturbances of Affective Contact", which marked the first time that autism was discussed in the professional literature.

Dr. Kanner provided case studies of 11 children in his paper. The children were between the ages of two and eight, and all of them faced some form of extreme social difficulties and exhibited strange usage of language along with obsessive behavior. Dr. Kanner noted that although some of the symptoms these children displayed were similar to those in children with schizophrenia, the disorders were not the same. He reported that schizophrenia in children is "preceded by at least two years of essentially average development; the histories specifically emphasize a more or less gradual change in the patient's behavior." He further said, "The children in our group have all shown their extreme aloofness from the very beginning of life, not responding to anything that comes to them from the outside world" (Kanner, 1943, p. 248). The children who display the severity of symptoms that Dr. Kanner spoke about are now considered to have "classic" autism. This is most probably what people think about when they hear a child has autism – that is to say the image of the child rocking back and forth, banging her head, flapping her hands and spinning objects, amongst other things.

In 1944 in Austria, Dr. Hans Asperger published a paper in which he described four children, who were his patients, with "autistic psychopathology." These children, all boys, were noted to lack empathy and engage in one-sided conversations along with having difficulty making friends, intense interests in peculiar topics and poor gross motor coordination. Dr. Asperger went on to describe these children as "little professors" because of their passionate interest in talking at great lengths about topics, regardless of others' interest in the subject.

Towards the end of World War II, Dr. Asperger opened a school to help these children. Unfortunately, the school was reportedly bombed, and a great deal of his early work was lost. It was not until 1981, when British psychiatrist Lorna Wing published the paper "Asperger's Syndrome: A Clinical Account" that Dr. Asperger's research became more widely known. Before that, not much of his work was translated into English from German. Dr. Asperger died in 1980 and never saw his work reach such prominence.

In 1987, the *Diagnostic and Statistical Manual of Mental Disorders, Third Edition–Revised (DSM-IIIR)* was published. At that time, the prevalence of autistic disorder was thought to be four or five children in every 10,000. The prevalence of pervasive developmental disorders, including both autistic disorder and Pervasive Developmental Disorder – Not Otherwise Specified (PDD-NOS), was estimated to be between 10 and 15 per 10,000 children.

In 1994, when the *Diagnostic and Statistical Manual of Mental Disorders, Fourth Edition (DSM-IV)* was published, the prevalence rates for autistic disorder were between 2 and 5 per 10,000. Therefore, at the most, only 1 in 2000 children was thought to have autism. Asperger's disorder was introduced into the field of mainstream mental health at this time, but there was not enough information to estimate its prevalence rates. Prevalence rates were also not provided for overall pervasive developmental disorders as they had been in the *DSM-IIIR*.

In 2000, the *Diagnostic and Statistical Manual of Mental Disorders – Fourth Edition – Text Revision (DSM-IV-TR)* was published. It was then noted "The median rate of Autistic Disorder in epidemiological studies is 5 cases per 10,000 individuals, with reported rates ranging from 2 to 20 cases per 10,000 individuals." There were no reported prevalence rates for either Asperger's disorder or PDD-NOS. In 2000, the Autism and Developmental Disabilities Monitoring Network (ADDM Network), a Centers for Disease Control and Prevention (CDC) project which is active in 11 states, found the average prevalence of the autism spectrum disorder (ASD) in 6 of those 11 sites to be 6.7 per 1000. Two years later, there were 14 sites in the ADDM Network at which data were being collected, and a prevalence rate of 6.6 per 1000 was found.

According to the 2007 data of the CDC, 1 in 150 eight-year-old children, in multiple areas of the United States, has an ASD. That would translate into 66 children per 10,000 and would be at least a 13-fold increase over the most liberal numbers reported in 1994. According to the website of the organization

Autism Speaks (www.Autismspeaks.org) a child is diagnosed with autism every 20 minutes. However, the number of the children (or teens, or adults) who have autism that goes undetected by well-meaning professionals who do not have the depth or breadth of knowledge or the experience necessary to appropriately identify the disorder remains elusive.

With the extreme growth in the number of children with ASDs, combined with the medical profession's improved ability to understand the range of symptoms which comprise the autism spectrum, significant steps need to be taken to educate today's professionals so that we do not miss the crucial developmental window to help these individuals. Much more can be done to assist a three-year-old child who has just been diagnosed with autism than a 13-year-old, or even a 31-year-old, who has been misidentified and misdiagnosed for years.

Chapter 2

The Importance of the
Autism Referral

In graduate school, I was trained to identify and diagnose the problems with which my patients present with. Psychologists are taught to do this through a combination of observation, interview and, at times, psychological testing instruments. In this process, we are taught to assume that the information we receive is presented in an open and honest manner through which it is seen that the patients and/or their family members are truly interested in understanding the cause of the presenting problem and the ways in which it can be remediated. While I believe this is the case for most evaluations, it is not always so when dealing with autism spectrum disorder (ASD). Because of that, several factors need to be taken into account before the first meeting with the patients and/or their parents.

Where Did the Referral for This Patient Come From?

This is a very important question that needs to be considered because it could have a direct impact upon the doctor's evaluation. A typical referral comes from the parents, requesting an evaluation for their child.

In my position at Kaiser-Permanente, I receive referrals from parents in one of two ways, either through a phone call directly from the parent (typically the mother, which will be discussed in greater depth later in this chapter) or through a professional, such as a pediatrician, speech therapist, neurologist or mental health professional, stating that they or the parents (or sometimes the patient, depending upon their age) are interested in an evaluation. These types of referrals typically indicate a significant amount of interest from the patients and/or their family in the evaluation. In these situations, it would be quite reasonable to believe that the patients and their parents would provide the examiner with a great deal of useful and factual information, necessary for an appropriate diagnosis.

I also receive referrals from care providers, such as the professionals mentioned above, in which the intent of the evaluation is not completely apparent, for one reason or another. There are times when the referring professional does not have a specific concern to articulate to the parent: "Well, Mrs. Smith, I don't really know why Ralph isn't talking [or banging his head against the wall, or wandering away from you whenever you take him outside], but it may be helpful for him to be seen by our specialist in that area." It may also be possible that the provider does not feel comfortable using the "A" word (autism or Asperger's) with the parents and simply says something to the effect of "I think it may be helpful for Ralph to be seen by a specialist. Luckily, we have such a person here in our clinic. I will make a referral for you if you would like."

When you meet parents who have been given a rather ambiguous referral, you may need to start out with rather general questions, or even "beat around the bush" for a while to obtain information about their understanding of why they are seeing you. I have found the following non-threatening statement to work well: "I received a referral from Dr. Jones about Johnny. What kinds of things are going on?" As the evaluation progresses, more information about the referring professional's, and the parent's, concerns becomes apparent. One can then proceed to ask more autism-spectrum-specific questions or get the parents to talk about those areas. If within the first minute the parents state, "Well, Dr. Gallo, I think Dr. Jones was concerned because I told him Johnny wasn't talking and doesn't have any friends," I think we know where this evaluation is headed.

It is quite common for parents to have different reactions with regard to a referral being made for their child. The following are examples of some types of parents one may encounter.

The reticent parents

Sometimes the most difficult referrals are those in which the parents have been told by the referring professionals about their concerns, but the parents do not agree with it. The following conversation exemplifies such a situation.

| Dr. Jones: | Mrs. Smith, all the information you told me today makes me concerned about the possibility that Ralph may have autism. I would like to have him seen by our specialist in that area to confirm that. |
| Mrs. Smith: | Well, I don't think he has autism, and I don't want a referral. |

The parents with pre-formed opinions

If the parents, or the patients, come to the evaluation with a preconceived notion about autism, such as "My child doesn't bang her head against the wall or spin plates, so she can't be autistic," they may be quite unlikely to listen to what you have to say. Much more on this topic will be presented throughout the book.

The parents in denial

These parents could present in a few different ways. One example would be a parent who comes to the evaluation and says that there is nothing wrong with their child and that they have no idea why the doctor wanted their child to be seen by a specialist for an evaluation. Another example could be a parent who doesn't want to know if there is a problem with their child – yet. They might think that if they viewed their child as "normal," then people, including themselves, would interact with him in a better manner and would be nicer to him. However, if they view the child as being disabled or "sick," it will make everyone, including the parent, sad, and their child will never be happy.

Have They Been Evaluated Previously? If So, by Whom?

In this day and age of increased awareness about mental and physical health issues, patients will often be seen by several professionals before coming to see a specialist. It is also possible that the family will have spent some time searching the Internet in an effort to obtain more information about whatever problem they think their child may have.

If you are seeing a very young child for an evaluation (one who is under the age of two) it is quite likely that the only professional they have seen in the past is their pediatrician. Quite often, the concern which first causes the parents to bring their son or daughter to the pediatrician is delayed speech. A "perfect world" scenario of this meeting with the pediatrician would go something like this: A mother brings her 18-month-old son to the pediatrician because he is not talking. The pediatrician shares the mother's concerns about the delayed speech and makes a referral to a pediatric speech pathologist. The speech pathologist, knowledgeable of the signs and symptoms of the autism spectrum, reports their observations and concerns to the mother and suggests that she take her son to a professional who specializes in ASDs to rule out such a disorder.

Unfortunately, that is often not the case. A more realistic, if somewhat negative, interaction would be the following: The mother takes her 18-month-old son,

Ralph, to the pediatrician because he is not talking. The pediatrician informs the mother that "boys tend to talk later than girls" (which is true) and tells her not to worry. The mother feels relieved because the pediatrician is the professional to whom she turns for answers. Since the doctor is not concerned, the mother is no longer concerned. The mother takes Ralph back to the pediatrician 6 months later and again 12 months later with the same concerns. Finally a referral is made to a speech pathologist. A referral to a Regional Center for a closer look at his language delay may also be made. (In California, Regional Centers are non-profit private corporations which contract with the Department of Developmental Services to provide or coordinate services and support for individuals with developmental disabilities. The Regional Centers are present throughout California as a local resource for individuals and their families. These facilities may have different names in other states, such as the Office of Mental Retardation and Developmental Disabilities in New York, the Agency for Persons with Disabilities in Florida and the Texas Department of Aging and Disability Services. Outside America, such centers may be called something else entirely.)

The speech pathologist who evaluates Ralph determines he is delayed in expressive and receptive language by a certain number of months. On the report, the speech therapist notes that Ralph did not make eye contact with her, only wanted to play with certain toys and became quite upset when redirected. The speech therapist may or may not mention these factors to the mother as additional areas of concern which warrant further evaluation. If Ralph were under the age of three, he could have been found eligible for services available at the Regional Center. If he were over the age of three, he could be referred to the local elementary school for an evaluation and be provided with services for his speech delay.

It may be a long time before Ralph would be seen by a professional who knows which signs and symptoms are suggestive of autism. It is also possible that the parents have obtained enough information on their own to suspect that their son may have autism and hence request an evaluation.

The older the individual becomes or the more impairing the symptoms are, the more likely it is that they will have been seen by several professionals, including speech and language pathologists, occupational therapists, psychologists, psychiatrists and neurologists. It is often seen that the parents get quite discouraged by this time and begin to doubt if the professionals would be able to determine what is wrong with Ralph. Three years ago, I met the mother of a 12-year-old boy, who came to the evaluation with a gym bag full of IEPs and numerous past evaluations of her son. You will be hearing more about this young man in forthcoming chapters. (IEP stands for Individualized Educational Plan and is basically a contract between the student and the school district with regard to the kind and extent of specialized services which will be provided to them to assist them in doing the best they can in school or, to use the educational code's catchwords, "to assess the curriculum." Autism is one of the many types of disabilities for which a child can be found eligible for services.)

Have They Already Been Evaluated for Autism?

This question actually comes up more often than one would think and has been a major reason for the creation of this book. There are times when astute parents bring their child to see a mental health or medical professional who does not have the necessary expertise to properly diagnose or rule out an ASD. There are a few questions which need to be asked, and answered, when seeing an individual who has already been assessed, regardless of the diagnosis.

Who was the evaluator, and what is their background with ASDs?

Let us say you have a wonderful internist whom you have been seeing for years and are very happy with. If you found that you needed brain surgery, would you ask the internist to perform the surgery? Of course not! Why? They are a doctor and went to medical school just like the neurosurgeon did. Hopefully, the reason you said no is because you do not expect them to be skilled in the area of brain surgery. If you were to go to a great Mexican restaurant for lunch and order Italian food, you would probably receive strange looks from the people behind the counter. The fact that the chefs in that kitchen make wonderful tacos does not mean that they know anything about minestrone soup or pasta primavera.

The same thing can be said for people diagnosing ASDs. There is no intensive specialty training program I am aware of for professionals to be qualified as "autism diagnosticians" or "autism experts." Therefore, you don't have any way of knowing the level of experience of the evaluator, unless you ask. Does the professional who saw your patient before you have expertise in diagnosing autism? What are the evaluator's credentials? How long have they been working in this field? How many evaluations have they conducted? Are they licensed as a mental health professional or as a medical professional? What was the parent's sense of this person? Did the parents like them and have confidence in them?

I have had the honor of meeting a few autism professionals about whom I know that they have a tremendous grasp of the spectrum. For example, if I were to see a child for an evaluation who was previously assessed by the director of the Autism Evaluation Clinic at the University of California at Los Angeles, I would feel fully confident that the conclusion which was reached was accurate. However, if the child were seen by someone whom the parents cannot even remember because the evaluation lasted for such a short period of time, I would have much less confidence in that conclusion.

There are times when you, as the objective diagnostician, may need to be wary of any ulterior motive the previous examiner may have had for determining that your patient does not have autism. If a child is being evaluated by an individual who works for an organization which would become financially responsible for providing services for the patient if they were found to have autism, that diagnosis could cost them a great deal of money. Conversely, if the child were found ineligible for services, by only having a language delay for example and not autism, then that organization could save significant sums of money. It would not be appropriate, in addition to being very upsetting for the parents, to be told that their child has autism, but the organization conducting the evaluation does not have any money for services right now. It would simply be much easier for the evaluators to inform the parents that their child does not have autism and therefore does not require any service. While this could sound like a story I am making up, I believe it may happen quite often.

On the other hand, there is another facet of the problem, which is still rather unpleasant and disconcerting: did the evaluator diagnose the child/teen/adult as not having autism because they simply did not have the depth of knowledge necessary to fully understand what to look for? An example of this could be an individual (such as a psychologist, a psychiatrist, or a developmental pediatrician) evaluating a 14-year-old boy who is on the higher functioning end of the spectrum. This boy frequently gets in trouble at school because of his desire to make friends. He is being used by peers who know he is quirky. The "friends" will tell him to approach a female classmate and make inappropriate comments, which they assure him the girl will think are funny. This student then has no idea how he could have sexually harassed a fellow student for which he is being expelled from school.

If the evaluator simply heard that this boy had friends and did not delve any deeper into the true nature of the friendships, they could assume that he is not on the spectrum, just socially naïve or maybe depressed. Maybe the evaluator did not even notice that the teen's eye contact throughout the evaluation was quite poor and that they were unable to sustain a reciprocal conversation.

What were the examiner's findings?

Did the examiner find the individual to have an ASD? Did they collect a sufficient history in enough detail to specify how they came to their conclusion? A few years ago, I evaluated a woman in her mid-30s who was found not to have autism because she was afraid of being alone. Somehow, her 30-year history of basically having no friends, significantly delayed language development and flapping her hands most of her life, in addition to numerous other symptoms, had been overlooked. It took me close to seven hours stretched over several meetings with numerous family members to obtain all the information I needed to make a diagnosis. The plethora of professionals she had previously met up with had spent significantly less time with her and came to a much different conclusion, namely that she was depressed and/or mentally retarded.

More than 1 year after completing this woman's evaluation, I was asked to testify at a hearing on her behalf at the Regional Center. Even with my in-depth evaluation, the Regional Center did not agree with the diagnosis of autism and refused to provide any service for her which would have helped improve her social skills, nor would they reimburse the family for their out-of-pocket expenses for paying for those services. After taking the stand for approximately an hour and talking about some potential reasons why she had gone undiagnosed for so long, the Regional Center was ordered by the judge to add the diagnosis of autism to her eligibility criteria. Needless to say, the family and I were very happy with that decision.

As a professional, it is difficult to give much credence to evaluations such as these, as you know that the examiner was only looking at certain problem areas and not the whole picture. However, to the parent, the patient or the layperson, all evaluations, no matter how flawed or inadequate, carry a great deal of weight. Most people do not know whom to believe when they receive such conflicting information. An evaluation by a medical or psychology graduate student may be just as meaningful as that of the chief of the department.

Do the parents and the patient agree with the diagnosis?

I am a firm believer in the fact that parents are *the* experts on their children and know if something is wrong with their child. It is unfortunate that we professionals are often not on the same page as the parents. If the examiner finds the individual to be on the autism spectrum and the parents and the patient, depending upon the age, agree, then we are doing well together and can work in a collaborative manner to find solutions. However, there are numerous times in which a diagnosis is made and the family wants a second opinion. In fact, this request may occur regardless of the diagnosis, as the parents could be told that the child is fine but they do not agree, or they could be told the child is on the spectrum and they still do not agree. This is a perfectly logical and an almost-expected part of the assessment by mental health and medical professionals.

A potentially confounding variable, which you as the provider of the first or second opinion may come across, is the parent's inability or unwillingness to accept or recognize their child's diagnosis. This fact cannot be stated strongly enough, because of its potential impact upon the outcome of the evaluation.

A few months ago, I received a phone call from a mother reminding me that I had seen both of her sons in the past and had diagnosed them with autism.

She said that at the time of the evaluation, she was in denial and didn't want to consider the possibility that I may be right. However, after several years of thought and a great deal of reading about the spectrum, she determined that I was correct. She asked for us to meet again to talk at greater length about how she can help her children, now that she is accepting of the diagnosis. We were finally able to talk about the problems her sons were having and what types of services would be beneficial for them.

In my 10 years of autism evaluations, I remember two mothers who had strong negative reactions to me. Both of those reactions came after I informed them that their sons were on the spectrum. One of the mothers, whom I saw again 2 years later, informed me that she had nothing against me at the time, but when she was in my office with her son for the evaluation and noticed the picture of my children, she felt that since my children were younger than her son, I must not have known what I was talking about. However, now that my children are older, she agrees with my diagnosis of her son. The other mother continues to fight against the diagnosis, even though the disorder has become so apparent that numerous other mental health professionals now clearly see her son as autistic as well. It is usually when the patient is an adult that they and their parents, if the parents are involved in the evaluation, are much more accepting of the diagnosis, as it then puts everything into perspective and explains a great number of issues in their lives.

Once the parents (or the patients) realize a diagnosis of an ASD may be made by examining the child's history, they might decide to "skew" that history or flat out "rewrite" it. If this were the case, they would no longer endorse the signs or symptoms of the behaviors which led to a diagnosis in the first place. As would be expected, it can be devastating to be told that your child has autism. Both the parents and the patients deal with that information in different ways, ranging from relief that their initial concerns have been justified to anger or hysterical crying. However, there are other parents who take a different approach and simply don't mention the information which qualified the child for a diagnosis in the first place. Examples of this occur from time to time when I am asked to conduct an examination for a second opinion. There have been times when I have asked the parents for information about such areas as when their child met his developmental milestones and who he played with in preschool only to be told that everything was fine with the child. However, when the child or teen was seen for the initial evaluation, it was reported that he did not talk until the age of three and mainly played by himself during preschool. There are several ways to delicately redirect parents down a more appropriate and helpful path. Examples of how to do so will be presented in later chapters.

One of the ways to determine if this rewriting of history is occurring during your assessment is to ask for copies of previous evaluations. If through your interview, the parents tell you that their son spoke on time and never lined up his toys, but on a previous report, it was noted that the parents stated their son was late in reaching his verbal milestones and had a habit of lining up all of his toy cars, you are presented with vast discrepancies which need to be looked into further. Talking with others who know the child well, such as teachers or day care providers, would be another way to obtain very helpful information, but this can only take place if the parents authorize such an exchange of information.

Once when I was testifying at a hearing, I was asked by the opposing counsel about the exact opposite of the situation that we are discussing here: "Would a parent ever falsely report a history in which their child appeared to have autism, even though they really don't?" I can only recall two situations, out of approximately 1,500, in which parents appeared to have either exaggerated or possibly fabricated symptoms in order to have their child diagnosed. Both situations involved the mother's mental illness. The mother with the gym bag full of previous evaluations, whom I mentioned earlier, endorsed numerous signs and symptoms of autism in her son, almost from birth. The information from the mother made me think that when I would meet this child, I would find that he was severely affected by autism. I thought that I would see someone who would not make any eye contact, would ignore me and would become obsessed with playing with toys. I was quite shocked when I met a very pleasant and socially agreeable pre-teen, who was nothing like what the mother had described. While I didn't ask the mother much about her history (including her mental health history) at the time of our first meeting, as she had so much information to tell me about her son, it appeared that her mental health problems played a significant role in how she viewed her son.

The other example I recall is a mother who also appeared to have mental health issues and was rearing her child in such a chaotic environment that it was basically impossible to determine where nurture stopped and nature took over. Was the child not socializing with others or playing with toys in an age-appropriate manner because the mother did not expose him to other children and rarely interacted with him, or was it because he had autism?

Who Is Attending the Evaluation?

Like many fathers, I work a great deal. As such, my wife is a significantly better historian of my children's developmental milestones and their daily activities than I am. She is the primary caretaker who often has most of these experiences with our children.

Back to our perfect world scenario in regard to assessments, when you conduct your evaluation, you would have both parents accompanying the child, and both of them would be quite knowledgeable and in agreement about their child's early development. It is important to point out that regardless of the individual's age, whether 18-month-old, 65-year-old or somewhere in between, you need to have another knowledgeable person to assume the role of the child's historian and provide you with the important information you need to appropriately conduct your interview.

A few years ago, my colleague and I met John, a 24-year-old man, at the request of his psychiatrist to determine if he has Asperger's disorder. John arrived 20 minutes late to the appointment, looking absolutely disheveled. We spoke for approximately 30 minutes about how he was doing and how he would like for us to be of assistance. Throughout our time together, John made very poor eye contact, had tremendous difficulty in conversing with us and gave off a rather "unusual" vibe. He was unable to tell us about his current daily routine, and it became quite apparent that he was unable to provide us with any information about his early childhood. I informed him that in order for us to help him to the best of our abilities, he would need to return for a follow-up appointment with one or both of his parents who could tell us about his childhood.

There are times when older patients, mostly teens and adults, are reluctant to have a historian, such as a parent or a sibling, accompany them to the evaluation. However, when I inform them that I need answers to questions such as how old they were when they began to talk, who their friends were in kindergarten and if they were a picky eater as a young child, they are stumped and realize the benefit of having their mom, dad or an older sibling accompany them. As previously mentioned, usually adults who are seen for autism evaluations are quite interested in the specialist's opinion and will be happy to provide access to whatever information and whomever is needed.

For the vast majority of evaluations I have conducted, either the mother brings the individual to the evaluation, or both parents are present. There have only been approximately two dozen times when the father brought the patient in alone. Around two thirds of those evaluations were very difficult to conduct because of the father's lack of knowledge of the child's early development. This statement is not meant to bash fathers in any way, especially since I am one myself. In general, fathers tend to be at work and outside of the home more than mothers, who are often the primary caretakers. Therefore, the main difficulty in this situation is that when it is only the father (or the nanny, the grandparent, the neighbor and the like) who brings the child to the evaluation, they often simply don't know the answers to the questions being asked. You, as the professional, need to feel comfortable telling that person, if necessary, that it would be more helpful to you, in order to properly do your job, to schedule another appointment when the mother (or another historian) can accompany them.

Another potential problem which I have noticed is the tendency for some fathers to be somewhat unwilling to identify or acknowledge the problems with their children. There could be cultural factors at work here as well, especially if the patient is a boy (as they are 75% of the time) or if the patient is the first or the only boy in the family. I have conducted hundreds of evaluations in which the mothers have told me that the father does not agree with the diagnosis.

Several years ago, I saw a young Asian boy who was affected by moderate to severe autism, who is unfortunately still stuck in this difficult position. The mother brought him to meet the autism team at Kaiser to learn about the services we could offer her and her son. During our almost two-hour meeting, the child spent all of his time wandering aimlessly around my office, flapping his hands and ripping sheets of paper into ever-smaller pieces. Despite numerous attempts by the mother to redirect him, this child would not engage in any other activity. He did not interact with the adults in the room, did not respond to any type of verbal or physical overtures by me or the case coordinator and would not play with any of the age-appropriate toys in the room.

It was quite obvious as soon as this child entered my office that he had autism. The mother reported that the father does not believe there is anything wrong with his son and had even had the child seen by a mental health professional from his country of origin, who agreed that the child did not have autism. The father felt that autism was an American problem and that we were imposing our mental health issues on to his son. In such a situation, the only person who loses is the child. This child was seen by a professional who was either biased in favor of the father or deeply unqualified, as has been shown by either their lack of knowledge about the autism spectrum or the inability to see beyond whatever story the father spun as a way to explain his son's unusual behavior.

The mother went on to say that the father was also attempting to prevent her from obtaining services for their son. I believe that that is hardly the mark of a good parent. However difficult it may be to accept that your child has a problem, no matter what the label is, the child's needs should come first, and the parents should not try to stop their children from getting the services they require. If nothing else, the father should be in agreement about his son's need for speech therapy, as he was three years old and not speaking at all.

Are the Parents, the Caregivers and/or the Patient Ready to Hear What You Have to Tell Them?

An interesting bit of information which often does not make it into most textbooks in graduate school is the response the parents and the patients have to the diagnosis of a disorder, or the lack thereof. Before the evaluation begins, there is no way to know what response you are going to receive if a diagnosis is made. Will they be relieved that someone has actually listened to and validated their concerns? Will they think that you don't know what you are talking about and discount both you and the diagnosis? Or will their reaction be somewhere in between?

There are times when the parents will not want to talk about the findings in front of the patient. I don't believe there is a right or a wrong way to convey this information, assuming that it is done in an appropriate, caring and professional manner. The level of reaction the patient exhibits, regardless of age, is often dependant upon how impaired they are by the autism. For example, imagine you are meeting an eight-year-old boy and his parents for an initial diagnostic evaluation. If the child is moderately affected by autism, it is likely that he will not have any reaction or even ask any question when you provide feedback to the parents. A child who has no reaction to the news and no reaction to his parent's reaction has just provided you with another important indicator that your diagnosis of autism is most probably correct. I think that it is often a good prognostic sign for the individual to have questions about the diagnosis or be aware of and respond appropriately to the parents' reaction. By displaying some interest in this process, which includes them and their well-being, it tells us that the patient is connected, at least to some extent, to the environment around them.

The professional reading this book should be somewhat surprised at the idea of a moderately affected eight-year-old boy coming in for an evaluation at such a late age. The majority of the emphasis placed on autism in the past several years has focused on early identification, which is wonderful, as we know that the earlier children with autism are identified and receive services, the greater the likelihood of them leading as productive and typical a life as possible. However, what about the older children who have "slipped through the cracks"? For that matter, what about those 20-year-olds and 30-year-olds who have never been identified and have simply been thought of as being quirky or odd? This book focuses on those populations in an attempt to identify them and provide help to all those who need it.

Chapter 3

How to Conduct the Evaluation

Who Is Needed for the Evaluation?

Three separate people are required for a comprehensive evaluation. The first person required, as simple and obvious as it may sound, is the patient. I mention this because there are times when parents may want to meet the examiner alone and not talk about their concerns in front of their child. This often comes up regardless of the fact that their child is three years old and will be too busy playing with the toys and objects in the doctor's office to care what the adults are talking about. If the patient is an adult, the parents might simply think it would be uncomfortable for them to be in the room.

There is no right or wrong way to handle the interview, but one needs to be considerate of the family's desires about how to proceed. More than a few years ago, I met a woman with a grown son who is on the spectrum. She told me that when he was younger and was taken by her to various doctor's appointments in an attempt to understand what was going on with him, she would have to answer the doctor's questions in front of him. As the interview would progress and the mother would talk more about her son's negative behaviors, he would become more depressed and sullen. The son later told the mother that he didn't know she thought he had such problems. I will present a solution to the dilemma of parents not wanting to talk in front of their children in the next section.

As has been previously noted, and will be discussed throughout the book, there are times when the parent's or the historian's information and recollections simply do not mesh with the patient's presentation. This is yet another reason why it is necessary for the individual who is being talked about to be part of the evaluation.

The second person required for a comprehensive evaluation is a parent or a very close relative. In the case of an adult patient, the input from a parent or a close relative is crucial. We have all had patients who will tell you they have lots of friends, are very social, and are happy as clams, among other things, when they obviously are not. Given the fact that the diagnosis of an ASD is made by history, the specialist needs to have the best historian available to assist in providing that history. As previously noted, with some exceptions, that person is typically the mother. There have been times when I have met patients in their thirties, forties, and fifties whose parents, typically the mothers, are still able to recall their children's early development.

I met a 30-something-year-old woman a few years ago, who was brought to see me by her older sister for an evaluation. This woman had a life-long history that truly exemplified autism. I told the two of them that I would like to meet additional family members, including the parents, to obtain as much background information as possible to solidify the diagnosis. The older sister warned me that talking with their parents may not be fruitful, as they are immigrants and believe that if they endorsed any sign or symptom of a problem with their daughter, she would be taken away and sent to an institution. Once I was able to talk with the parents about their concerns and assure them that that was not the case, I was rewarded with a plethora of useful information.

It is often quite helpful to have the parents or the patient, depending upon their age, sign a "Release of Information" form allowing the specialist to talk with other individuals who could provide additional, necessary information. For young children, these could be nannies, grandparents, preschool teachers, and the like. For teens, we could talk with teachers, coaches, and employers. For adults, one could speak to siblings, spouses, coworkers, and clergy, among others.

The third person necessary to complete our diagnostic triad is a well-trained professional who has a well-developed, experienced grasp of the autism spectrum and all of its complexities. As I mentioned earlier, this person does not have to be a child psychiatrist, child psychologist, pediatrician, developmental pediatrician, or pediatric neurologist. I know of several non-doctoral professionals who have an excellent grasp of the spectrum and whose opinion I trust implicitly. However, given the severity of the diagnosis, most parents appear to be more willing to accept the news if it comes from a professional who carries the title of "doctor."

The diagnostician conducting this evaluation needs to be aware of how ASDs manifest throughout the lifespan. They should have seen enough individuals on the spectrum to have a comprehensive grasp of the various manifestations of the disorder. This fact leads very well into the next component of what makes up an appropriate evaluation.

What about Screening Teams?

Within the Kaiser Permanente system in Southern California, I know of several different ways in which autism evaluations are conducted, all with their own pros and cons. For example, our ASD diagnostic service is set up in such a manner that two days a week, the autism case coordinator Sue Bassett, a licensed clinical social worker, and I conduct approximately four evaluations; two of the other three days a week, Sue is with our developmental pediatrician while she conducts additional ASD evaluations. Her fifth work day is spent writing progress notes and meeting with parents. If the patients require evaluations by a pediatric neurologist, speech therapist, occupational therapist, psychiatrist, or any other professional, then these evaluations are conducted at a separate time and typically with that professional alone.

In other facilities, there are various team approaches in which a pediatric neurologist, speech therapist, occupational therapist, and the case coordinator basically function as a "tag team" with the child and the family. One set of two professionals meets with the patient alone to conduct the evaluation and observe their behavior, while the other set of two meets with the parents to obtain background information. After a certain amount of time, they switch. They then discuss the case after the family has gone home, and they later have the family return for feedback. The approach in other facilities and probably the most common approach is to simply have a case coordinator, developmental pediatrician, or psychologist conduct the evaluation on their own.

During the time in which Sue and I conduct our evaluations, we usually meet the patient and the parents together to obtain information while interacting with and observing the client in the same room. We are then able to conduct our evaluation, compare notes between the two of us, and provide the parents and the patient with feedback all in the same appointment. I believe that there are several beneficial aspects about working in teams. First and foremost is the obvious fact that there is another professional in the room who might notice actions or behaviors in the patient one might have missed. There have been numerous times during evaluations when Sue picked up on repetitive hand or body gestures or some type of intense fascination with a toy that I did not see as I talked with the parents.

There are times when the patient may feel more comfortable with one evaluator over another. This allows one of us to ask the parents questions, while the other pays more attention to and interacts with the child. This type of interaction with the patient is very important for several reasons. One is that the specialist is able to observe the individual's response when strangers initiate interactions with them. One often has very different interactions with children who are suspected of being on the spectrum when they are asked to engage in activities that might not interest them, such as talking to the evaluator, than when they are simply allowed to do whatever they want while the evaluator talks to their parents.

An example of this could be in a team assessment with a preschool-aged child. Typically, we would allow the child to have some time to wander around the office and examine their new surroundings. During this time, we would ask the parents questions and observe the child. It is possible, if not likely, that the child would play with the toys, keep themselves busy, and appear to be having a fine time. However, when the time seems right, Sue or I would call the child's name, ask them if they were having a good time, or ask them to do something for Sue, such as giving her a toy or drawing something for her. It could be a sign of autism if you have a child who is perfectly happy doing their own thing and then becomes very upset or completely ignores you when called upon to interact.

Making attempts to engage with the child while noting the responses that are received can be quite helpful in the overall evaluation. Of course, you need to keep in mind the fact that the member of your team, or yourself if you are conducting the evaluation alone, is not the child's peer, and it is often quite common for children on the spectrum to interact well with adults. There have been innumerable times in which parents have taken their child for an evaluation only to be told their child does not have autism because they interacted well with the examiner. This type of poor understanding of the spectrum is something that needs to be corrected. Children on the autistic spectrum may interact well with adults but remain on the periphery with peers.

Behavioral observations noted during the examiner's attempts to interact with the child can be very helpful in bringing to the parent's attention the inconsistencies between what they are reporting and what we as examiners are seeing. Consider the following example: During an evaluation of a young child and his parents, you notice the child does not look at you when you call his name and spends a great deal of time flapping his hands. When you mention this to the parents, they state that he engages in those behaviors quite often, which is causing them a great deal of concern. In that situation, your behavioral observations of the child are consistent with the parents' reports. Another example, using the same type of family dynamic, would be the parents stating that they have never seen their son do that before or have seen him do so only rarely. In that situation, additional consideration needs to be given to some of the points mentioned in the previous chapter, such as the specific reasons for the parents to be here, their concerns, and their openness to hear what the specialist has to say.

In just a one-week period during the writing of this book, I met two separate families whom I had previously seen for evaluations years ago when their sons were three or four years old. At the time of our initial meetings, the parents did not endorse enough signs or symptoms of autism to warrant a diagnosis. However, years later, they contacted me to inform me of their concerns about their children having autism. When I discussed their children's histories with them, as reported to me at the time of our first meeting, no problems were noted. However, during our second meeting, significant problems in development that were not previously endorsed were discussed.

In fact, one of the mothers simply stated that four years ago, she could not handle the thought of her son having autism and therefore did not answer my questions truthfully. It was only after she had years to think about the situation and realize the true problems her son was having that she was able to come to terms with the fact and admit to herself that her son had autism. It is sad to think about all of the services these children could have received and all the progress they could have made if the parents had come to terms with their children's difficulties years earlier.

Another benefit of a diagnostic team is made apparent when the parents do not feel comfortable talking in front of their child. In those situations, Sue and I split up; I talk with the parents in another room, while Sue stays in the evaluation room to interact with the child. Once all of my questions have been asked and answered, we reconvene and compare notes. In this manner, the parents tend to be happy, as they feel that both their and their children's feelings were taken into consideration. This also provides the diagnostic team a large amount of time, possibly up to one hour, to have a team member interact with the child in a one-on-one setting.

Quite often, professionals from various disciplines are included in a diagnostic team. Speech therapists, occupational therapists, psychiatrists, and neurologists may all participate. While these are invaluable professions and a very helpful part of the overall evaluation of the child, I don't believe they are completely necessary for making an *initial* diagnosis. Before I upset and alienate my readers from those professions, let me elaborate with an example.

Imagine an evaluation is being conducted with a three-year-old boy who was referred by his pediatrician because of speech delay, isolating himself at preschool, and his habit of putting his hands over his ears in reaction to loud noises. Given the fact that you know from the outset that his speech is delayed, it would be unnecessary for him to have a speech evaluation *prior* to a diagnosis being made. It would definitely be helpful to know how delayed his speech is and if he has a receptive language delay as well, but that could be conducted after the evaluation. Overall, I think a speech and language evaluation should be conducted at a later time, as it would provide the treatment team with valuable information.

The same would be said for an occupational therapy/sensory integration (OT/SI) evaluation for this child. The referral states that he covers his ears when he hears loud noises. If further questioning reveals significant sensory, fine motor, or gross motor problems, an evaluation and input from the OT/SI therapist would be a very helpful and integral part of treatment, but it does not need to be conducted *prior* to a diagnostic evaluation, as it is already known from talking to the parents that the child has sensory issues.

What about Screening Tools?

I find that some parents and professionals have very interesting preconceived notions about what "testing" for an ASD should entail. There are times when the parents will say, "You didn't really 'test' my child for autism at all. You just asked me a bunch of questions and interacted with them." There are no blood tests that can be conducted or pencil-and-paper tests for children or infants to fill out in order for an evaluation to be conducted. If we take into consideration that autism is a disorder that is diagnosed based on history, obtaining that history can be done in several ways.

I am rather fond of analogies and metaphors and use them often in evaluations and explanations with parents and patients. When parents ask me what type of testing will be conducted during their child's evaluation, I tell them that I will ask them a great deal of questions about their child's early development and the time they were in kindergarten, in addition to observing and interacting with their child. When they ask what specific tests will be used, I tell them my clinical interview and observations are typically all that are needed, but we can use more formal measures as necessary. I let them know that my diagnostic interview covers the same key points as some of the more complex measures and that we can do it in less time. As an analogy, I often ask them that if they could go to a doctor and get a thorough evaluation that lasted for two hours or one that lasted for five hours but still gave the same results as the two-hour one, which one would they choose? As would be expected, if both evaluations were just as thorough, they would pick the one that disrupts their lives the least.

There are also professionals and parents who have a misguided, or uninformed, notion that autism cannot be diagnosed without the use of formal quantitative instruments. If all mental health disorders required a full psychological evaluation before being diagnosed, then it would mean that every individual, regardless of age, who has ever been diagnosed by their primary care doctor, a licensed clinical social worker, a marriage and family therapist, or a psychiatrist has not been properly diagnosed because no formal psychological testing instruments were used. That is just plain silly and calls into question every provider's knowledge about the disorders they treat, as it suggests that they don't have the necessary knowledge to appropriately diagnose their patients.

At times, professionals who do not have a great deal of knowledge about the depth and breadth of the spectrum will perform autism evaluations. One way to conduct an evaluation if you do not have a tremendous amount of experience with that population is to rely quite heavily on various autism screening tools, such as the Childhood Autism Rating Scale, the Gilliam Autism Rating Scale, and the Modified Checklist for Autism in Toddlers, to name a few. While I do not mean to disparage these helpful instruments in any way and think they can be a very useful accompaniment in an evaluator's arsenal, I would warn against relying too heavily upon them or using them as the sole source of information for evaluation, as there are numerous factors that need to be taken into consideration when using these instruments.

First and foremost, who is the person completing the test? Is it the mother who is interested in the evaluation and inclined to answer truthfully? Is it the father who is not really sure why he is completing the form and may be unable to recall his child's early development? Maybe it is completed by both parents who are quite frightened of the prospect of there being anything wrong with their child and do not want to acknowledge their child's problems for whatever reason. If it is not known for sure that the individual completing the questionnaire is providing factual information, the instrument could be useless at best or harmful at worst. These are the reasons why one needs to have a comprehensive grasp of the spectrum, in order to truly know what the questions are aiming for and then be able to relate that information with the parents in such a way that they understand it as well.

Second, what is the parent's reading level and understanding of the questions? If English is not the parent's native language, is there anyone available to translate it for them? For that matter, if there is a translator available, do they fully understand the questions they are translating? While the questions on these instruments are not written in a complex fashion, there are times when the parent's understanding of the question is different from the test creator's idea. For example, years ago I had a parent complete one of the screening tools in the waiting room before the evaluation. When I received it back from her, I went over all the questions she had marked in a problematic fashion. The form I used had two questions that asked something to the effect of "When your child was four to five years old, did they nod their head to mean yes and shake their head to mean no?" The parent checked the "No" box for both. When I asked her about this, she stated that her child did not nod his head to mean yes or shake his head to mean no – he simply told her yes and no.

The problem here is that the mother and the person who created the instrument were not viewing the question in the same way. The mother felt that by answering no she was reporting developmentally appropriate behavior. However, I believe the question was really looking at the child's ability to get their wishes and desires met in a nonverbal manner, but that was not how the parent understood it. Had the mother's answer not been clarified, it would have been an erroneous sign suggesting that the child might be on the autism spectrum.

I often find it helpful to have the parent complete a screening instrument before we meet, but for subtler reasons than would be expected. I tend to look not specifically at which questions the parents reported in a problematic fashion but at the overall picture the parent's answers present.

Allow me to explain further. Let's say I have a referral from a pediatrician or other professional in which a number of problematic behaviors are reported, such as the child not having any friends, making poor eye contact with others, and being obsessed with trains. I then have the parents complete a screening questionnaire in the waiting room. When I receive the questionnaire back from the parent, minimal to no problems are reported. If that were the case, I would know right away that there is a disconnect somewhere between the referring party's view of the child and the parent's. Conversely, if the instrument denotes numerous problems that the parents are concerned about, I can reasonably expect the parents to be open in talking with me about their child's difficulties.

This approach is also quite helpful at times when the child has already been diagnosed as having an ASD and the parents are coming for a second opinion. If a diagnosis has already been made and the parents are only acknowledging a few problematic signs on the initial questionnaire, I know that I am going to need to look very closely at the information being provided to me and compare what the parents report with what the first evaluator has noted.

When the parents and the patient arrive, I like to go out to the waiting room to meet them, introduce myself, and give them the screening questionnaire to fill out. At this time I do some very quick and preliminary "waiting room diagnosing." There are basically two ways in which this interaction occurs. Just think about what happens when you go out to the waiting room or walk into the examining room to meet a new patient. You walk out and say something to the effect of "Hi. I'm Dr. Smith. Nice to meet you." You then stick out your hand that they shake, and then the evaluation proceeds from that point forth.

There have been numerous times when I will go to the waiting room, call the person's name, and walk over. I then typically look at the parents, say, "Hi. I'm Dr. Gallo. Nice to meet you," and shake their hand. When I say hello to the patient, I also like to shake their hand. When I am doing this, I notice if the patient is looking at me or not and if they shake my hand or not. From a young age in our society, children are taught to look at a person when they are introduced to them and to shake the other person's hand with their right hand. There have been many times when I have put my hand out to shake and the patient, regardless of age, has looked at the floor, mumbled hello, and shaken my hand with their left hand as if their wrist were broken. Needless to say, this type of unusual interaction does not mean that they have autism, and having a very socially appropriate handshake with good eye contact does not mean that they are not autistic, but it is one more additional piece of information that can begin to help me build as complete an evaluation as possible.

I have unfortunately read numerous reports in which it was reported and met several parents who have also reported that the evaluator had the parent complete two or three screening instruments and asked a few questions; that's it. That examiner is relying too heavily on those instruments to do their job for them and not enough on their own understanding of autism to come up with an accurate diagnosis.

More Comprehensive Assessment Devices

The Autism Diagnostic Observation Schedule and the Autism Diagnostic Interview–Revised

The Autism Diagnostic Observation Schedule or ADOS and the Autism Diagnostic Interview–Revised or ADI-R are two "gold standard" instruments used in autism research and evaluations that require and deserve attention. While both of these instruments are very impressive and very useful and definitely have their place in an evaluation, there are both pros and cons to their use and how heavily one relies upon them. As with most instruments in science, the results depend on the skill and the experience of the rater.

For those not familiar with it, the ADOS is basically a structured interaction with the individual. For younger children and when some of the earlier modules are being used, at least one of the child's parents sits in and may be called upon to assist during parts of the evaluation.

The ADOS consists of four modules, one of which is used depending upon the patient's expressive language ability. Typically, as the patient grows and develops their language more, they move up to a higher module that has more verbal interaction and less playing. The ADOS can be incredibly helpful in some situations, such as when the diagnosis is unclear or when the examiner believes the child is on the spectrum but the parent or the caregiver, for whatever reason, has not provided the history necessary to support such a diagnosis.

There have been a great number of instances in which Sue and I (or I by myself) have met children and their families for evaluations and have been unclear if the child was on the spectrum. We would administer the ADOS in the hopes of obtaining additional clarifying information. There have been numerous times when during the initial evaluation the child appeared very pleasant and happy to wander around my office. Once we began the ADOS, however, and the child was asked to stop doing whatever it was that they were doing and start doing what

I wanted them to do, the problems became more apparent. In such cases, the previously easy-going and happy child may now become upset, possibly because they do not want to interact with you. When the child is placed in a rather structured situation, more of their true functioning, such as poor eye contact, lack of imaginative play, and poor pragmatic language, becomes apparent.

Another positive aspect of the ADOS, as previously mentioned, is when the evaluator's observations of the child, teen, or adult just does not mesh with what the historian has reported. As previously noted, typically at least one parent stays in the room for the administration of the ADOS. If one is meeting a teen or an adult, it is usually not necessary to have the parent present.

Let's say that during your clinical interview of the parents, they tell you their child usually responds appropriately when their name is called and engages in creative play at home. However, during the ADOS, all of your attempts to interact with the child, or even to get him to look at you when you call his name, are in vain. When you attempt to engage him in playing with various toys, he becomes much too fixated on your pen or watching the wheels of cars move back and forth to interact with you in the slightest. It becomes quite difficult for the parents to "not see" the types of behavior their child is engaging in. Utilizing the ADOS also takes the evaluation beyond just what the parents would view as "your opinion" and provides them with quantifiable evidence to support your hypothesis.

Another very helpful aspect of the ADOS in keeping with the point just noted is its ability to offer quantifiable information. When you write a report in which quantifiable information is included, it is much more difficult for others to disagree with your findings. If your primary care doctor shows you an X-ray in which it is very clear, in black and white, that you have a broken bone, there is very little room for disagreement.

A drawback of the ADOS is that it only provides a snapshot of the individual for that period of time during which it is administered. For example, if you were to meet a child who is severely affected by autism (socializes poorly, has limited eye contact, has some type of intense fascination, and so on), those behaviors should be quite evident during your time together and would be scored as such on this instrument. However, the results could be different if you were to assess a child or a teenager who is higher functioning or is less affected by the spectrum. If you were to put that child or teen in a semi-structured setting with an adult, it is possible that they would "keep it together" for the 45–60 minutes that the ADOS takes to be administered. This is a reason why the creators of the ADOS note that it is a classification and not a diagnostic tool and should not be used as the sole basis for evaluation.

The ADI-R is another wonderful tool that like the ADOS provides the examiner with quantifiable information to be used in making a diagnosis. The only potential drawback of this instrument is the length of time it requires to administer. There are 93 items that need to be asked of the parents or the caregiver and can take between three and four hours to complete. However, once that has been accomplished, especially when using the ADOS and the ADI-R in tandem, the findings become very difficult, if not impossible, to refute.

There have been instances in which I have reviewed reports by other professionals that have quite a long list of all of the instruments that were utilized in the assessment. When I see that the child has been administered an ADOS, an ADI-R, a Vineland-II, and an IQ test, I think that the evaluation could have taken up to six hours total, with approximately two hours with the patient (for the ADOS and the IQ test) and the rest of the time with the parents (for the ADI-R and the Vineland-II). However, there have been numerous parents who tell me that the entire evaluation took only two hours. If the parents are correct, there is no way that all of those instruments were administered correctly in that period of time, which would call into question the validity of the findings. I always find it helpful to ask the parents about the previous evaluation.

IQ and cognitive assessment

With the advent of new and revised cognitive and developmental assessment devices, we are better able to assess individuals of all ages in these areas. However, I am not aware of many assessment devices that have norms for the autistic population. Administering standardized psychological tests to either individuals on the autistic spectrum or people whom you think might be on the spectrum could be a somewhat questionable undertaking. For example, if a standardized IQ test, such as the Wechsler Intelligence Scale for Children–Fourth Edition (WISC-IV) or the Wechsler Adult Intelligence Scale–Third Edition (WAIS-III) were utilized with an autistic individual, you would be giving a standardized test to a nonstandardized individual.

In the *WISC-IV Administration and Scoring Manual*,[1] it is noted that "it is important not to attribute low performance on a cognitive test to low intellectual ability when, in fact, it may be attributable to physical, language, or sensory difficulties. Depending on the nature of the difficulty and the test administered, the child's performance may result in scores that underestimate intellectual capacity if the test is administered in the standard fashion" (Wechsler, 2003, p. 11).

It may be difficult to determine if the IQ score obtained is an accurate representation of the individual's true level of functioning, or if their autism and its accompanying difficulties have played a role in under-representing their true level of functioning. The norms of these IQ tests are based on a more "neurotypical" population, providing more confidence in their validity and reliability when used with that population, as opposed to individuals on the autism spectrum.

---

[1] *Wechsler Intelligence Scale for Children®, Fourth Edition (WISC®–IV)*. Copyright © 2003 NCS Pearson, Inc. Reproduced with permission. All rights reserved.

I am not suggesting here that such tests should not be used with individuals on the spectrum but that we should simply keep in mind that there might be more variability in their scores than in those within the normative population. It is possible that an approach as straightforward as using the 90% confidence interval, instead of the 95% confidence interval, which I typically use, would mostly resolve this issue. I should note that there is no research at this time I am aware of that explores this hypothesis.

While entire chapters, if not complete books, could be written about this topic of administering IQ tests to individuals on the autistic spectrum, my only wish in bringing this topic to light is that either the psychologist who administers the test or the professional who reads the report that includes the test data should keep this idea of increased score variability and the possibility of the score being an under-representation in mind.

Including an IQ test (or other type of cognitive measure) as part of an autism evaluation is in keeping with the "Best Practice Guidelines for the Screening, Diagnosis and Assessment of Autistic Spectrum Disorders" (a report by the state of California's Department of Developmental Services to provide recommendations for professionals about how to assess for ASDs), at least in California. The information obtained from the IQ test also helps to paint a more comprehensive picture of the individual being evaluated, in terms of their areas of strength and weakness. With that being said, I professionally do not view an IQ test as a necessary part of an autism evaluation.

Let me provide a few examples to support my position:

(1) You meet a six-year-old boy and his parents for an evaluation, and the parents endorse all the *DSM-IV-TR* criteria you need to support a diagnosis of autism. How would an IQ test change the parents' information? If the child is also mentally retarded, then that diagnosis would not override the autism diagnosis but could provide you with additional information. The mental retardation alone would not be the reason why the child does not have any interest in peers or spends a great deal of time flapping his hands.

(2) You meet a preschooler and his parents for an evaluation. The family was referred to you because of the child's expressive-language delay and shyness. The in-depth information you obtain from the parents and the teachers, possibly including an ADOS or even going to the preschool to observe the child, does not support a diagnosis of autism. If you administer some type of cognitive or intellectual measure to the child, the score you receive is still not going to change the fact that none of the adults who know that child well reported the necessary signs and symptoms for a diagnosis. However, it would provide you with additional, non-autism-related information.

The information obtained from administering an IQ test in these two examples is somewhat helpful in the overall picture of these children but does not change anything in terms of the diagnosis. It could be more helpful in terms of treatment planning, but that is outside the scope of this book.

Projective tests

On the Rorschach inkblot test, there is a special score called "autistic logic," which is a significant indicator of schizophrenia. According to Exner and Weiner's classic text, *The Rorschach: A Comprehensive System, Volume 3: Assessment of Children and Adolescents, Second Edition,* "[w]hen autistic subjects are not mentally retarded, however, examiners should be aware that relatively high functioning autistic persons when tested as adults have been found to show many schizophrenic features on the Rorschach, including indications of disordered thinking" (Exner and Weiner, 1994, p. 152). This finding needs to be kept in mind by those psychologists who may want to administer a Rorschach when assessing for autism.

Can a Thorough Evaluation Be Conducted in the Office?

I believe the answer to this is a resounding yes. If a knowledgeable historian accompanies the patient and they are seen by an evaluator with an in-depth knowledge of the disorder, I believe a comprehensive evaluation can be conducted in the office. With that said, I am always of the impression that the more information and more history that can be obtained, the better.

Therefore, if you are meeting a child of elementary-school age or younger and are able (with the parent's permission) to observe the child at school or at the park, then that would be very helpful in providing you with additional information. That way, you are not relying solely upon other people's interpretation of how, or if at all, the child is playing with others; you are able to see it for yourself. However, given today's society, with managed care, insurance reimbursement rates, and the need to have a packed schedule, it could be rather unlikely that the diagnosing professional would be able to leave the office to observe the child. It may be helpful if, in the future, an observation was considered an integral component of an evaluation.

Observations become more complex and complicated as the patient gets older for a couple of factors, not the least of which is the fact that simply observing someone changes their behavior. Obviously, if the teen or adult patient were impaired by their autism to such an extent that they would not notice you observing them, then you really would not need to go out and observe them in the first place, as the answer to your diagnostic question would be rather obvious. Second, if the patient is an adult, do they have a job? If so, would you be able to quietly observe them at work, without letting anyone else know the true reason why you are there and without possibly causing the patient any embarrassment?

How Long Do You Need to Spend with the Patient and/or the Family to Conduct a Comprehensive Evaluation?

There is a story about when Abraham Lincoln was a lawyer and two friends came to him and said, "Lincoln, we want you to settle an argument for us. Tell us exactly how long a man's legs should be." It just so happened that one of the two men had very short legs, while the other had very long legs. "Hmmm," Lincoln said. "I never gave this matter much thought. But now that I think of it, I would say . . . a man's legs should be exactly long enough to reach from his body to the ground."

Keeping with our late president's wisdom, an autism evaluation needs to last as long as it takes in order to answer the referral question. There have been instances in which a parent has brought their child in for an evaluation and the first words out of their mouth are something to the effect of "Thank goodness we are meeting up with you. My four-year-old son doesn't talk at all, flaps his hands all day, and does not have any interest in playing with other children." While, of course, additional information is required, you are pretty much on your way to solidifying a diagnosis in less than 1 minute. However, there are also times when I have had two or three meetings with patients and their parents for several hours apiece, administered several psychological tests, and talked with numerous additional people only to determine that they did not have an ASD.

You need to become comfortable taking all the time you need to answer the question in front of you: does this individual have an ASD? If you meet the patient and their parents for two hours and still do not feel comfortable answering that question, then don't answer it. Feel free to ask them to allow you to talk with anyone else whom they think could provide you with necessary information. Having more than one meeting can also be helpful, as it allows you to see how the individual's behavior changes as they become more comfortable with you.

The possibility that you cannot answer the referral question (at this time) with 100% confidence should also be considered. I recently met a two and half-year-old boy and his family for an evaluation. At first, the parents reported their son is not very social and only speaks a few words. From the beginning, I was presented with information that was suggestive of autism. However, as the evaluation progressed and I asked more questions, I became less sure.

The parents reported that their son is cared for by another family member 12 hours a day while they are at work. The aunt who takes care of him does not have any children of her own for her nephew to interact with. When the parents pick him up after work, he typically does not go to bed until midnight and tends to be allowed to do whatever he wants. The parents reported that when they are at home with their child, he usually watches television or is on the Internet while they do chores.

It was very difficult to determine the underlying causes of this child's difficulties. Was he not socializing with others because he had autism or because he has minimal interactions with peers and even less interaction with his parents? Could his speech problem be a sign of autism or just an expressive-language delay exacerbated by him being spoken to in two different languages, mainly by the television and not by his parents?

I concluded the evaluation by telling the parents about the concerns I have in regard to autism and that the reasons for his difficulties were not clear enough to me to make a diagnosis. I recommended that they spend more quality time with their son, at least 30 minutes a day, without the television or the computer on, that they get him on a more typical sleep schedule, and that they contact the Regional Center for a speech evaluation. It is quite likely the child will be provided with Center-based speech therapy, which will also expose him to other children. I suggested that if the problems continued after six months of these interventions, they should return for us to look further into the possibility of autism. I never heard back from the family and hope that it was because they listened to my advice and implemented the steps I suggested with the result that the problems resolved themselves.

Chapter 4

Information to Gather at the Outset of the Evaluation

As you can imagine, one does not start an evaluation by saying, "Hi, I'm Dr. Gallo; does your child have any friends? How is the eye contact?" Or by asking, "Does your child like to spin objects?" It is important for everyone to feel comfortable at first and then start off slowly by developing a good rapport with both the patient and parents; this approach will serve you well as the evaluation proceeds.

The Parent's Awareness of the Problem

Once everyone is in the office and we have concluded our small talk (e.g., "Did you find the office OK?" and "Hopefully traffic wasn't too bad"), I will often begin the evaluation by saying something to the effect of "I received a referral from Dr. Creel and he has some concerns about Ralph. What kinds of things are going on?" The types of answers you receive from the parents at that time can be very revealing and will let you know in what direction the evaluation is headed. For example, the parents might say, "Well, Ralph is six years old and he didn't start talking until he was almost two, and his first grade teacher is concerned about his ability to focus in class and play with others." The concerns reported by parents sound quite logical and merit further exploration.

There are times when the family might start off by reporting less problematic behaviors of their child; especially if they are unclear about the true purpose of the evaluation. They may say, "Well, Dr. Creel wanted us to come and see you because Ralph was being very defiant and would not do the things we asked him to do." In those situations, when the parents' main concerns which brought them to the evaluation are not autism related, I find it helpful to read the referral from the doctor to the parents so that we all know the types of issues we will be focusing on.

My favorite types of referrals are those which come from the parents directly because of their concerns about their child having autism. Such referrals make you feel more confident that the parents are very much interested in finding out what is going on with their child and will be willing to provide you with all the information you need to be as thorough as possible.

What Has Been Done So Far?

Before discussing autism-specific information, you would like to know what the parent's and patient's concerns are and what, if anything, has been done in the past to ameliorate those concerns. If the patient is a school-aged child, has the child received an evaluation from the school? Does the child have an IEP, 504 plan, or any other type of accommodation in the classroom? According to the US Department of Education's website,[1]

> Section 504 is a federal law designed to protect the rights of individuals with disabilities in programs and activities that receive federal funds from the U.S. Department of Education (ED). Section 504 provides: "No otherwise qualified individual with a disability in the United States ... shall solely by reason of her or his disability, be excluded from the participation in, be denied the benefits of, or be subjected to discrimination under any program or activity receiving Federal financial assistance ... "

If the child has an IEP with the school, what has the testing for the IEP found? It would be very helpful for the parents to provide you with a copy of the IEP and any testing which accompanies it, such as psycho-educational assessments, speech evaluations, and occupational or physical therapy evaluations. Does the IEP find the child eligible for any special educational services? If so, which ones? Is the school concerned about the same issues which the parents and patient are?

If the patient is either under the age of three or past high school age, is the child a Regional Center client? If so, what services is the child receiving or has received in the past? Typically, between these ages, the school district plays the primary role in providing services and it is usually before or after these ages that the Regional Center provides more services.

Do people other than the parents have concerns? Are there other family members who have concerns? When the child was young (if he or she is not

---

[1] U.S. Department of Education, Office for Civil Rights, *Free Appropriate Public Education for Students With Disabilities: Requirements Under Section 504 of the Rehabilitation Act of 1973*, Washington, D.C., 2007.

young at the time of the evaluation) did others, such as teachers, family members or even strangers, express concern? What are the child's report cards like? Is the child earning good grades? I have often found that teacher comments on progress reports can be very helpful. Teacher comments such as "Roland socializes too much in class with his neighbor" and "Sally needs to work on making friends and socializing with her peers during free play time" can be very revealing.

If the patient is an adolescent or adult, is he or she employed? If so, what is the job description, how long has he or she worked there and how is it going? If the patient is not employed, why not? Has the patient been employed in the past? If so, why did the patient leave the former job? Was he or she fired or asked to leave the job? Has the patient been diagnosed with any other mental illness? If not formally, has there been concern about him or her having a mental illness? With there being a great deal of overlap between autism and ADHD, the diagnosis specifically merits further exploration to determine if we are looking at only ADHD, only autism or a combination of the two. This is only a partial list of the ideas which should get the diagnostic ball rolling.

Is There Any Relevant Pregnancy or Medical History?

How was the mother's pregnancy? Were there any problems or complications with the pregnancy? Was the baby born on time? Was the baby healthy? What were the infant's APGAR scores? How much did the baby weigh and how long was the baby at birth? If the parents tell you that their child was born 3 months premature, weighing 1.5 pounds, the information is quite significant and can play an important role in diagnosis. I believe all of this information is relevant because it help provide us with the overall picture we are looking for. I am sure that there is a multitude of information already published about how problems or complications *in utero* can have an effect upon prevalence rates of autism; however, that is beyond the scope of this book. I simply want to have this information to determine if I should have the child be seen by another professional, such as a developmental pediatrician or a pediatric neurologist, to know if these problems could somehow either present similarly to autism or potentially be the cause of the problems we are looking at.

Does the patient have any medical problems? Could there be any underlying medical issues which could be causing or exacerbating the patient's problems? I saw a pre-teen girl in the past who the doctor thought had autism. When I reviewed her medical history, it was found that she had agenesis of the corpus callosum. This condition is a rare birth defect in which the corpus callosum, which connects the two hemispheres of the brain, does not develop normally. Research suggests that social difficulties can be an effect of this condition and these difficulties have often been misdiagnosed as part of an autism spectrum disorder. Due to the fact that I was able to review this child's medical chart, I steered away from making a diagnosis.

This is often one of those interesting questions where patients and parents tend to give a knee jerk reaction of "No" and need some gentle prodding to assist them in delving deeper into the recesses of their memories. You will find the need to engage in this type of gentle prodding throughout these evaluations.

I will often ask more specific questions to help jog their memories: "Any major illnesses, such as accidents, head injuries, seizures, surgeries, broken bones, allergies, asthma, ear infections, anything like that?" With autism-specific evaluations, you may also want to determine if the patient has undergone any chromosomal tests, DNA or Fragile X screens. In my experience, it has been quite rare that a child whom I have diagnosed has had Fragile X or a chromosomal or genetic problem; it is always good to enquire.

It almost goes without saying that if, during your evaluation, it is divulged that around the time when the child's language regressed, the child also suffered a major car accident, resulting in a week-long coma (or something similar), the information is highly relevant and can take your evaluation in a drastically different direction. One interesting offshoot of naming all these various medical problems is that the parents have often totally forgotten about these medical problems until these are mentioned by name. There have been numerous instances in which parents will tell me that their child has always been perfectly healthy, only to remember 10 minutes later the numerous medical problems that the child had when he or she was younger. Although it is feasible that whatever minor medical issues the patient may have in early childhood are not playing any role in their possible autism, it is always best to just be as thorough as you can.

A young boy was referred to me because of temper tantrums and a loss of previously acquired skills. When I asked the parents if their son had undergone a medical and/or neurological work-up, they stated that one was scheduled for the next week. When I heard back from the parents after the medical evaluation, they reported having found numerous medical and neurological issues underlying the problems their child was having. If this information was not obtained, I could have looked very foolish for diagnosing him with a mental health problem, when the real cause was purely medical.

It is very important to ask about the individual's hearing and if it has ever been assessed. One of the many Dr. Gallo's Pearls of Wisdom mentioned throughout the book is that parents of children on the spectrum often take the child to the pediatrician because of their concern that their child may be deaf or have a hearing problem. However, when the evaluation or audiogram is complete, it is determined that the child's hearing is perfectly normal. With children who are on the spectrum, I often hear parents say that their children are "in their own world," that they are often "spacing out" and doing their own things, including not reacting when their parents call their name.

Developmental Milestones

The information you obtain here is crucial in appropriately conducting your evaluation. At the very least, you need to enquire about language development, motor milestones and toilet training.

Linguistic milestones

You need to be very specific in your questions in this area and need to obtain relatively exact answers from the parents. The question "Did your son talk on time?" followed by "Yes" is not sufficient. There is no way of knowing if your professional opinion of "on time" is the same as that of the parent's. What if the parent has several children, none of whom spoke until the age of three, so since the child you are evaluating did not speak until the age of three, the parents consider that normal? Perhaps, this is the parents' first child and they have been told that it is normal for boys to talk late; therefore, once again, it is normal that their children did not speak their first word until the age of 2 1/2.

Typically, by 12 months, a child should say at least one to two words. By 18 months, their vocabulary should have increased to as many as 20 words. By the age of two, they should be saying several single words and two- to four-word sentences. Between two and three years of age, a child should be able to verbally identify various body parts, combine nouns and verbs and have a vocabulary of around 400–500 words. Between three and four years of age, the child should be able to tell a story, create sentences of four to five words and have a vocabulary of approximately 1000 words.

The specific questions you need to ask would include: "What was your child's first word?" "At what age did the child speak his or her first word?" "When did the child first start putting two words together?" "What were the child's first sentences?" "When did the child put three words together to make a sentence?" "When did the child begin to speak in a way that was understandable by a person other than a family member?"

By asking these open-ended questions, you are helping the parents to recall this important information. By asking them specifics, such as their child's first words, we can obtain additional information beyond simple linguistics. What I mean by this is that a child's first word tends to be something rather common, such as "mama, dada, ball, dog, up, no." If the child's first word was something rather unique, such as "concrete" or "gutter," that is rather unusual and merits further exploration. While it is possible that saying "gutter" as your first word means absolutely nothing and is just quirky, it could also be an early indicator of a child's intense focus on that object. This information could then provide you with information relevant to the next chapter.

Motor milestones

While the linguistic milestones are diagnostically significant, the child's motor milestones, once again, help to paint the comprehensive and all encompassing picture we are looking for. Although it is not necessarily the case, children on the autism spectrum tend to have more fine and gross motor delays than other children.

When did the child sit up, crawl and walk? If the child is old enough to hold a pencil or ride a bike, how are those skills progressing? What about the child's gross motor and fine motor coordination? Again, you may need to ask the patient and parents very specific questions to get the required information. Do they draw with crayons? Do they hold a pen properly? Do they tend to be clumsy? Do they trip and fall often? Do they tend to step on your feet and not be aware of having done so? This factor tends to come up often with children on the spectrum and can be related to sensory integration issues, which will be discussed in another chapter.

Toilet training

Considering that boys tend to toilet train later than girls and that 2 1/2 to 3 1/2 are the normal age ranges for children to acquire this skill, you want to find out when the child became toilet trained, both for urination and defecation and both during the day and at night. Although it is not terribly uncommon for children to have toileting accidents, did the patient have accidents? Is the patient still having accidents? Are these at night or during the day? Urine or feces? Have any medical conditions been identified or ruled out which could be causing or exacerbating this problem? What is the child's reaction to the accidents? Once again, delayed or absent toilet training is not a diagnostic sign of autism, but it is important to know for the overall picture of the child, as it is not uncommon for individuals on the spectrum to have had toileting issues earlier in life.

Chapter 5

Diagnostic Criteria for the Autism Spectrum Disorders

In the *DSM-IV-TR*, under "Disorders Usually First Diagnosed in Infancy, Child-hood, or Adolescence," five pervasive developmental disorders are listed: autistic disorder, Rett's disorder, childhood disintegrative disorder, Asperger's disorder, and PDD-NOS (including atypical autism).[1]

With this "newer" mindset of looking at ASDs, we are only going to focus on the three most common disorders, namely, autistic disorder, Asperger's disorder, and PDD-NOS.

The *DSM-IV-TR* diagnostic criteria for each of these disorders are as follows.

Autistic Disorder

A: A total of six (or more) items from (1), (2), and (3), with at least two from (1), and one each from (2) and (3):
   (1) Qualitative impairment in social interaction, as manifested by at least two of the following:
      (a) Marked impairment in the use of multiple nonverbal behaviors such as eye-to-eye gaze, facial expression, body postures, and gestures to regulate social interaction.
      (b) Failure to develop peer relationships appropriate to developmental level.

---

[1]Reprinted with permission from the *Diagnostic and Statistical Manual of Mental Disorders, Text Revision, Fourth Edition* (Copyright 2000). American Psychiatric Association.

(c) A lack of spontaneous seeking to share enjoyment, interests, or achievements with other people (e.g., by a lack of showing, bringing, or pointing out objects of interest).

(d) Lack of social or emotional reciprocity.

(2) Qualitative impairments in communication as manifested by at least one of the following:

(a) Delay in, or total lack of, the development of spoken language (not accompanied by an attempt to compensate through alternative modes of communication such as gestures or mime).

(b) In individuals with adequate speech, marked impairment in the ability to initiate or sustain a conversation with others.

(c) Stereotyped and repetitive use of language or idiosyncratic language.

(d) Lack of varied, spontaneous make-believe play or social imitative play appropriate to developmental level.

(3) Restrictive repetitive and stereotyped patterns of behavior, interests, and activities, as manifested by at least one of the following:

(a) Encompassing preoccupation with one or more stereotyped and restricted patterns of interest that is abnormal either in intensity or focus.

(b) Apparently inflexible adherence to specific, nonfunctional routines or rituals.

(c) Stereotyped and repetitive motor mannerisms (e.g. hand or finger flapping or twisting, or complex whole-body movements).

(d) Persistent preoccupation with parts of objects.

B: Delays or abnormal functioning in at least one of the following areas, with onset prior to age three years: (1) social interaction, (2) language as used in social communication, or (3) symbolic or imaginative play.

C: The disturbance is not better accounted for by Rett's Disorder or Childhood Disintegrative Disorder.

Asperger's disorder

A: Qualitative impairment in social interaction, as manifested by at least two of the following:

(1) Marked impairment in the use of multiple nonverbal behaviors such as eye-to-eye gaze, facial expression, body postures, and gestures to regulate social interaction.

(2) Failure to develop peer relationships appropriate to developmental level.

(3) A lack of spontaneous seeking to share enjoyment, interests, or achievements with other people (e.g., by a lack of showing, bringing, or pointing out objects of interest to other people).

(4) Lack of social or emotional reciprocity.

B: Restricted repetitive and stereotyped patterns of behavior, interests, and activities, as manifested by at least one of the following:
  (1) Encompassing preoccupation with one or more stereotyped and restricted patterns of interest that is abnormal either in intensity or focus.
  (2) Apparently inflexible adherence to specific, non-functional routines or rituals.
  (3) Stereotyped and repetitive motor mannerisms (e.g., hand or finger flapping or twisting, or complex whole-body movements).
  (4) Persistent preoccupation with parts of objects.
C: The disturbance causes clinically significant impairment in social, occupational, or other important areas of functioning.
D: There is no clinically significant general delay in language (e.g., single words used by age two years, communicative phrases used by age three years).
E: There is no clinically significant delay in cognitive development or in the development of age-appropriate self-helps skills, adaptive behavior (other than social interaction), and curiosity about the environment in childhood.
F: Criteria are not met for another Pervasive Developmental Disorder or Schizophrenia.

Pervasive Developmental Disorder Not Otherwise Specified or PDD-NOS (Including Atypical Autism)

While there are no specific diagnostic criteria for PDD-NOS, as there are for autism and Asperger's, some troublesome signs and symptoms are definitely present. The *DSM-IV-TR* states, "This category should be used when there is a severe and pervasive impairment in the development of reciprocal social interaction associated with impairment in either verbal or nonverbal communication skills, or with the presence of stereotyped behavior, interests, and activities, but the criteria are not met for a specific Pervasive Developmental Disorder, Schizophrenia, Schizotypal Personality Disorder, or Avoidant Personality Disorder. For example, this category includes 'atypical autism' – presentations that do not meet the criteria for Autistic Disorder because of late age at onset, atypical symptomatology, or sub-threshold symptomatology, or all of these."

As noted, this diagnosis can be given when the individual definitely shows signs and symptoms of being "on the spectrum" but does not meet all of the diagnostic criteria. An example would be a child who is only displaying one problematic social sign, in addition to the behavioral symptoms. This child could be a preschooler who does not have difficulty with eye contact, will show and bring things that interest him to others, and will do nice things for others but does not have any interest in playing with others, isolates himself from peers, and is obsessed with Thomas the Train.

Another example would be a teenager who meets all of the diagnostic criteria for autism in terms of the social, language, and behavioral difficulties, but those difficulties are not at a terribly problematic level and do not cause a tremendous amount of angst for the individual. This may be seen in the teachers not noticing any problems but the parents being concerned about their son's continued quirky and asocial behavior that is causing some difficulty at home.

Although I do not consider either Rett's disorder or childhood disintegrative disorder to be ASDs, I will include their diagnostic criteria here because of the fact that they are noted to be disorders that need to be ruled out in order for a diagnosis of autism to be made.

Rett's Disorder

A: All of the following:
    (1) Apparently normal prenatal and perinatal development.
    (2) Apparently normal psychomotor development through the first five months after birth.
    (3) Normal head circumference at birth.
B: Onset of all of the following after the period of normal development:
    (1) Deceleration of head growth between ages 5 and 48 months.
    (2) Loss of previously acquired purposeful hand skills between ages 5 and 30 months with the subsequent development of stereotyped hand movements (e.g., hand wringing or hand washing).
    (3) Loss of social engagement early in the course (although often social interaction develops later).
    (4) Appearance of poorly coordinated gait or trunk movements.
    (5) Severely impaired expressive and receptive language development with severe psychomotor retardation.

Childhood Disintegrative Disorder

A: Apparently normal development for at least the first 2 years after birth as manifested by the presence of age-appropriate verbal and nonverbal communication, social relationships, play, and adaptive behavior.
B: Clinically significant loss of previously acquired skills (before age 10 years) in at least two of the following areas:
    (1) Expressive or receptive language
    (2) Social skills or adaptive behavior
    (3) Bowel or bladder control
    (4) Play
    (5) Motor skills

C: Abnormalities of functioning in at least two of the following areas:
  (1) Qualitative impairment in social interaction (e.g., impairment in non-verbal behaviors, failure to develop peer relationships, lack of social or emotional reciprocity).
  (2) Qualitative impairments in communication (e.g., delay or lack of spoken language, inability to initiate or sustain a conversation, stereotyped and repetitive use of language, lack of varied make-believe play).
  (3) Restricted, repetitive, and stereotyped patterns of behavior, interests, and activities, including motor stereotypes and mannerisms.
D: The disturbance is not better accounted for by another specific Pervasive Developmental Disorder or by Schizophrenia.

Chapter 6

The Main Problem Areas of Autism: Social Impairment

My father once told me that if you truly have an in-depth understanding of a subject, no matter how complex or complicated it may be, you should be able to explain it in simple and straightforward terms to basically anyone. This brings me to a brief story of the first time I met an individual on the autism spectrum, or so I thought.

Soon after earning my Ph.D., but before I was licensed, I worked at a residential treatment facility for teenage girls. I was the psychologist in charge of conducting assessments on the new residents. One day, I met a 13-year-old, very tall, and pretty Hispanic girl whom I will call Maria. Maria was quite a diagnostic conundrum. She was sent to residential treatment for acting out sexually, running away from home, and stealing from her family. After I exhausted my typical battery of psychological tests, such as projectives and personality and IQ tests, all of the evidence appeared to support a diagnosis of a bipolar disorder, but something else seemed to be going on. As I flipped through the *DSM-IV*, I came across Asperger's disorder, something I knew basically nothing about, but as I read more, the criteria appeared to fit well.

I then contacted Maria's mother to obtain more background information. Given the fact that the mother and I probably had the same level of knowledge about Asperger's, I basically read the diagnostic criteria to her from the *DSM-IV* and asked if that sounded like her daughter. When the mother endorsed the requisite number of symptoms, I added Asperger's disorder to her multiaxial diagnosis and wrote my report, content that I had identified the problem.

About 1 week later, I ran into the psychiatrist for the facility, who had a couple of choice words for me. She informed me that she had trained with Dr. So-and-So at XYZ University who is an expert on ASDs and that Maria definitely does not have Asperger's. The doctor accurately noted that Maria was much too socially appropriate and does not display any true signs of the disorder. Needless to say, I was pretty embarrassed. However, looking back all those years, the psychiatrist was correct, and my absolute lack of knowledge about the spectrum really threw off my ability to appropriately diagnose this teen.

I include this story as an example to stress that diagnosing these disorders is rather complex, and the information offered by parents, such as Maria's mother, can only be properly utilized for diagnostic purposes if the examiner truly knows what they are looking for.

As the title of this chapter suggests, entire chapters are dedicated to each of the three problem areas necessary for a diagnosis of autism. (Only two of these areas, socialization and behavior, are necessary for a diagnosis of Asperger's disorder.) Information related to the diagnosing of teens and adults will be included in their respective chapters.

The *DSM-IV-TR* for both Autistic Disorder and Asperger's disorder, requires "[a] qualitative impairment in social interaction, as manifested by at least two of the following: A: Marked impairment in the use of multiple nonverbal behaviors such as eye-to-eye gaze, facial expression, body postures, and gestures to regulate social interaction. B: Failure to develop peer relationships appropriate to developmental level. C: A lack of spontaneous seeking to share enjoyment, interests, or achievements with other people (e.g., by a lack of showing, bringing, or pointing out objects of interest) or D: Lack of social or emotional reciprocity."

Let's tackle each of these criteria one at a time.

Marked Impairment in the Use of Multiple Nonverbal Behaviors to Regulate Social Interaction

While this category includes several issues, one of the main possible impairments here is also one of the historically significant traits of autism, namely, a lack of appropriate eye contact. Both professionals and lay people alike tend to have a preconceived notion that all individuals with autism have poor eye contact and that if an individual's eye contact with others is poor, they must be autistic.

Before even beginning to ask questions, an evaluator needs to always keep in mind criterion B in the diagnosis of Autistic Disorder: "Delays or abnormal functioning in at least one of the following areas, with onset prior to age three years: (1) social interaction, (2) language as used in social communication, or (3) symbolic or imaginative play." This means that in order for a diagnosis of an ASD to be made, these problem areas need to have been issues for the individual basically all of their life. Therefore, if the person in your office is 12 years old and makes good eye contact with you when you shake their hand and looks at you appropriately throughout the evaluation, you may be missing an important piece of the puzzle. Is the child engaging in these socially appropriate interactions because his parents have drilled these skills into him day in and day out for the past 12 years?

How were all of these behaviors before the age of three? I usually ask the parents or caregivers if the child attended preschool or daycare before being enrolled in kindergarten. If so, I try to get them to think back so that we can focus mainly around that time, plus or minus a year, for the majority of the evaluation. We also need to keep in mind that autism is a remitting disorder; it gets better as time progresses. Given the fact that we are all exposed to social interactions on a daily, if not hourly, basis, it would make sense for these appropriate social skills to continue to improve with time.

Let's say you are evaluating a young child, between the age of three and five, and ask the parents, "How is Johnny's eye contact?" They may tell you that he has always made good eye contact with them and that it has never been a problem. With that said, does he look at you (the examiner) during the evaluation? Sometimes the parents will tell you the individual's eye contact is poor, especially when he knows he did something wrong, or that he makes really good eye contact with them but not with others. It is a pretty typical human response for children to not look into a person's eyes when they are being scolded.

Does the child always look at mom and dad without fail but does not look at anybody else? Does the child look at you throughout the evaluation when you are trying to interact with them as some type of peek-a-boo or hiding game? In those situations, these behaviors become more significant. We need to keep in mind that mom and dad hold a very special place with children and that they are the people the children feel the most comfortable with. Just because a child makes good eye contact with their parents is not enough information to conclude that they make good eye contact overall.

Dr. Gallo's Pearl of Wisdom: The fact that a parent reports that they took their child to the doctor and an audiologist at a very early age because they thought he was deaf is quite significant and could be indicative of an ASD, especially if the results reported that his hearing is normal. Quite often, the main reason for this evaluation was because their child would not look at them when they called his name.

Consider this hypothetical exchange between an examiner and the parents of a 12-year-old brought in for an evaluation.

Dr. Gallo: How is Ralph's eye contact?
Mother: His eye contact is fine with me.
Dr. Gallo: Does he look at you when you talk to him?
Mother: Yes.

That sounds pretty cut-and-dried and could allow you to move on to the next question. However, let's take a more comprehensive look at Ralph's eye contact and spend more time on the topic.

Dr. Gallo: How is Ralph's eye contact?
Mother: His eye contact is fine with me.
Dr. Gallo: Does he look at you when you talk to him?
Mother: Yes.
Dr. Gallo: Great! Has it always been that way with him?
Mother: No, we really had to work on that with him. When he was younger, we had to say to him all the time, "Ralph, look at me when I am talking to you." There were even times when we had to physically move his head in order for him to look at us.

This is an example of how just taking the information given by the patients or their parents at face value, without doing additional digging, can lead in the wrong direction. This is also a good example of the remitting nature of ASDs and how some of these problems can be overcome, in addition to how the presentation of these areas of difficulty changes over time.

Another factor of eye gaze, which is more difficult to measure, is modulation. For example, how does one differentiate between lovingly gazing into another person's eyes and staring at them? There was talk among veterans of a "1000-yard stare" in which a soldier is not really seeing you but is seeing beyond you. I use this as an example to illustrate the idea that when the individual is looking at you, they may not be really seeing you. Are they truly looking into your eyes, or at your forehead, or somewhere two inches above and to the left of your head?

This is a poignant example of how individuals, even those severely affected by autism, can be taught to look at people when they speak to them, but the subtler aspects of eye contact, such as modulating their gaze, may escape them. Therefore, asking parents if their child tends to stare at people would also be a good question. How is the individual doing in regard to eye contact and modulation of gaze during the evaluation? Are they staring at you? Your patient's behaviors and interaction with you during the evaluation are incredibly important and should be given the appropriate amount of diagnostic weight.

In 2002, research was conducted by Klin and colleagues in which children with autism watched clips of the movie *Who's Afraid of Virginia Woolf?* and an infared camera recorded the trajectory of their eye gaze. This research found that children on the spectrum tended to look at people's mouths and various objects on the screen twice as often as neurotypical children. The children on the spectrum were also found to look at the eyes of the actors only half as much as neurotypical children do.

It would be helpful to ask the parents if their child looks at them when they call their name. If they do now, did they do so when they were younger? This is asked about in the ADI-R and is also one of the scoring criteria on the ADOS. Going back to my "Pearl of Wisdom," problems with eye contact and responding when their name is called could have been a key factor for why the child was taken for an audiological evaluation in the past. What was your impression of the patient when you met them in the waiting room? Did they look at you then?

It is not uncommon that as more specialized questions are asked of the parents, such as if their child looked at them when they called his name, they simply don't know the answer because they have never thought about it. If the child is having problems in daycare or if there were (or currently are) marital problems in the home, it is quite likely that the parents will not remember their toddler's interest in looking at them the first time they called his name. However, if the patient is still a child, you could ask the parents to think about that, observe their child in those situations, and let you know the next time you meet.

In fact, having appointments spread out over a period of time, and possibly even over separate locations, could be quite helpful, as it assists the patient in becoming more at ease with you and increases the likelihood of them engaging in more of their "typical" behaviors. There are times during shorter evaluations, or with parents who are not ready to hear what you have to say, when the parents (and occasionally the patients) disagree with your findings on the basis that you only spent X number of minutes with them and because their child did not act as they usually do as they were in an unfamiliar setting. By meeting more than once and even going to the patient's home, school or daycare, you can drastically reduce that as a confounding variable.

I will also typically ask the parents, after about an hour or so, if the behavior I have been observing is typical for their child. If I am meeting a child who has been to the doctor recently and was given a few shots, they may be more reluctant to interact with me out of fear of getting another shot. Maybe the child did not sleep well the night before, has a cold, or has not had their morning or afternoon snack yet. All of that information is important to know.

If I met a child who ignored me and had temper tantrums during the evaluation, I would ask the parents if this was his typical behavior. If they reported that he was typically very mellow but was just diagnosed with a major ear infection and was in significant pain, then that information would be important to be taken under consideration when incorporating my behavioral observations with the information the parents have provided. However, if the parents tell me that that is Johnny's typical behavior at home, then that is diagnostically relevant.

Another quite complicated factor of nonverbal behavior is the child's ability to understand nonverbal cues and body language. This ability develops with time and experience and is rather difficult to assess with very young children. That is another reason why all of the questions asked by the examiner need to keep

returning to the time when the child was around the preschool/kinder-
garten/first-grade age. By the end of that age range, the child is old enough
to understand body language but is probably not yet old enough to be in the teen
or preteen period of not caring.

About five years ago, I was having lunch with two fellow psychologists at a local
Mexican restaurant by the clinic where we work. After lunch, as we were getting in
my colleague's car to leave, I noticed a young man, who did not look very happy,
walking toward one end of the parking lot. A few seconds later, I looked over
toward where he was headed and saw another rather unhappy-looking young
man, around the same age, walking toward the first guy. For whatever reason,
I was able to read their body language and knew that they were going to fight
and that we should get out of there. Unfortunately, my two coworkers, who are
very bright and well educated people, were oblivious to this fact, even after I
told them we needed to get out of there right away. It was not until the two men
started fighting and were rolling around on the ground 50 feet from us that my
coworkers realized the urgency of the situation. How was it that I knew there was
going to be a fight and my coworkers had no clue?

This is an example of being able to read nonverbal cues and body language,
something individuals on the spectrum often have difficulty doing. Some of the
more typical questions you would want to ask parents, or the patients themselves,
depending upon their age, would include "Is Ralph able to read facial expressions
and body language?" Unfortunately, the most typical response I get to this
question is a blank look. That is a reason why one often needs to rely on numerous
examples and the ability to rephrase the question in several ways.

Dr. Gallo: Is Ralph able to read nonverbal behavior and body language?
Mother: I think. What do you mean?
Dr. Gallo: Is he able to tell how people are feeling or what their moods are without
that person having to tell him?
Mother: I'm not sure. How would I know that?
Dr. Gallo: Well, how about this. How long have you and and his father been
together?
Mother: Ten years, why?
Dr. Gallo: Well, you have known his father for a long time. When he comes home
from a hard day at work and is tired or annoyed or just plain worn
out, are you able to tell that by the way he walks in the door, or by how
he is breathing, or the look on his face?
Mother: Yes.
Dr. Gallo: OK, great. That is an example of you reading nonverbal cues and body
language. Do you think your son is able to pick up those cues as well?
Mother: Oh, now I understand. No, I don't think he gets that.

I often like to ask parents, "If you were lying on the couch and watching a sad
movie or if you were on the phone and received some bad news and were a little

teary eyed when your child walked in the room, would he notice?" This provides the parent with another concrete and real-life example to think about, as this is something that happens to everyone from time to time.

A concern that also needs to be kept at the back of your mind while examining such an individual is that the individual's ability to read their parent's body language and being able to read a stranger's or a peer's body language is very different. Don't forget that children are around their parents, especially when young, most of their waking time. Therefore, it makes sense that they would be able to determine their parent's moods just by looking at them, but it would be much more difficult to decode another person's body language.

I often ask the parents, "Let's say I was in a bad mood and the tone of my voice changed while we were talking, or I crossed my arms over my chest or gave you an unhappy look. I would imagine that even though we never met before an hour ago, you would be able to tell from my body language that I was unhappy about something. Do you think your child would be able to read those cues as well?"

Personal space can also be an issue with children on the spectrum, as they often do not have a good sense of what constitutes appropriate personal space. For example, when you meet a patient for a therapy session or an evaluation, you are probably sitting about 6 feet or so away from them. You are aware of this "personal space bubble" in which getting too close to another person would make them feel uncomfortable, making them want to back up. Oftentimes, children and adults on the spectrum do not have a clear grasp of this concept and become what I call "space invaders."

Does the child you are meeting show an awareness of this personal space, or do they get right "in your face" to talk to you or show you something? This is a behavior that, if present during the interview, can be very telling and should be noted in the observation section of the report. While you are interacting with a child, if they come over to talk to you and stand 3 inches away from your face, then this behavior would answer this question very well. There may also be times when a child will want to show you something and will put it right up to your nose to show it to you, without any idea that it is too close and that you cannot see it properly.

Children who are sensory seeking may also engage in certain types of inappropriate behaviors. A young boy I recently saw liked the feel of pantyhose, which his kindergarten teacher also used to wear. As you could imagine, this did not go over well with her. Some children on the spectrum may also have such an intense interest in things that this interest, once again, would be another cause of their poor sense of personal space. An example of this would be a child who really enjoys feeling soft textures and walks up to women on the street, or in the mall, and starts touching their silk blouse or their hair. While this could be somewhat easier to explain if it is a young child doing this, it would cause a significant problem if it were a teenager or adult trying to touch a stranger's blouse.

The ability to read body language and nonverbal cues also plays an important role in the upcoming section regarding having an intense preoccupation with something. For example, if the individual is obsessed with weed whackers and that is all they want to talk about, are they able to tell from the other person's face that they are not interested in that topic and do not want to hear or talk about it? We will discuss this topic in great detail in Chapter 8.

Failure to Develop Peer Relationships Appropriate to the Developmental Level

This is a very complicated topic, as this problem manifests itself differently, depending upon the age of the individual being assessed. Therefore, let's start in chronological order.

With a great deal of emphasis now being placed on identifying children on the autism spectrum as early as possible, you, the specialist, will probably see a large number of preschool-aged children. It is not uncommon to see three- and four-year-olds often, with even some two-year-olds from time to time. Some very important questions that need to be answered early in the evaluation include the following: Is the patient an only child? Are they enrolled in daycare or preschool? Do they go to "Mommy and Me" or any type of "Gymboree" class? These questions need to be asked and answered in order to determine the extent to which they are provided with social interactions with others.

It is important to differentiate between a typical "slow-to-warm" child and a child on the spectrum. Let's use a typical, shy three-year-old child who does not have any siblings as an example. If the mother were to bring that child to preschool or daycare, it could be quite normal for the child to be rather shy at first and not to seek out other children to play with. Maybe he or she wants to play with the other children but is more content to watch. Perhaps they will engage in developmentally appropriate parallel play in which they do the same thing the other child is doing, in the same general vicinity as the other child, but not with them.

Oftentimes, problems manifest themselves as the mother brings the child to daycare or preschool. Instead of being "slow-to-warm," they never warm up. The child does not seek out others to ask them to play, is not interested in other children, and does not respond well to peers who approach him. This second example could be somewhat more suggestive of having an ASD than the first example.

One of my favorite socialization questions to ask that provides a great deal of information is "When Johnny was around three years old and was taken to the park to play, what would he do?" This is one of those instances in which the parents typically respond with "He played." That answer is incredibly general and really does not tell us anything diagnostically useful. Significantly more specific information about how the child played needs to be obtained. Did he play on the equipment? Did he sit in the sand for a half an hour and watch sand run through his fingers? Did he hunt for bugs? Did he include the parent in his play? Would he interact with other children? Would he seek out other children to play with? Would he approach others? What did he do if another child approached him? The answers to these questions provide us with a great deal of relevant information.

Dr. Gallo: When Johnny was very young, around the age of three, and you would take him to the park on a sunny weekend afternoon, what would he do?
Mother: He would play, just like everybody else at the park.
Dr. Gallo: OK. How would he play? What did he do?
Mother: He would play on the swings and on the monkey bars. Johnny really also liked to play in the sand.

If you were to stop inquiring at that point, you would have not obtained any new, useful, or important information about this child's social interactions. You would need to dig deeper.

Dr. Gallo: Would Johnny play with other children?
Mother: No.
Dr. Gallo: Would he seek out other children at the park?
Mother: No, he mainly kept to himself.
Dr. Gallo: What would happen if other children approached him?
Mother: He might play with them, depending upon the type of toys they had and if they wanted to do what he was doing.
Dr. Gallo: Do you think Johnny was more interested in playing with the children who approached him or with their toys?
Mother: Mostly their toys.
Dr. Gallo: How long would Johnny play with these children?
Mother: It would usually not be more than 5 minutes before somebody was crying or there was some problem.

It is always beneficial to observe the child in an environment such as a public park or an indoor play area at a mall if the child being evaluated is around preschool age and you are able to observe them in such surroundings. That could be as typical of an observation as can be made at that age range. When the child gets older and attends school, the playground is another wonderful environment to observe them in. Some of the behaviors that need to be observed include the following: Is the child playing with same-aged peers or talking with the adults? Are they seeking others out? Are they responding appropriately when other children approach them? Are they engaging in any unusual or stereotypical behaviors? If you are within earshot, it could be helpful to find out if the child is talking to his or her peers, and if so, what are they talking about?

Dr. Gallo's Pearl of Wisdom: When the parents tell you that all of their child's "friends" are either significantly older or younger than they are, then it is a matter of concern. This often happens because children much younger than your patient look up to him or her and will probably do whatever he or she wants them to do. Individuals much older than the patient, including teenagers and adults, will typically do what the patient wants them to do for a period of time because they probably think that the patient is cute or a nice kid. With children on the autistic spectrum, there is the high likelihood that the patient is unable to compromise with same-aged peers. This often causes friction, as the peer may or may not want to do what the patient is doing. Also, the peer may be aware at some level that the patient is "quirky" or not really relating well with them. For the sake of diagnostic clarity, it should also be noted that this issue can occur with children who have ADHD.

Preschool

In a daycare or preschool setting, there are numerous other children who are around the patient's age. You will want to know if the child plays with them or if he is off "doing his own thing." At the Mommy and Me or Gymboree class, is the child interested in their peers, or are they more interested in the various objects or toys scattered around the room? If the child is verbal, do they have friends whom they can name and like to play with?

Dr. Gallo's Pearl of Wisdom: When a parent tells you that their child has numerous friends at school, but the child cannot remember any of their names, then it is a matter of concern.

Kindergarten

When you are seeing a kindergarten or elementary school child, you now have more life experiences to draw from when talking to the parents. The main questions in this section are as follows.

Does the child have peer relationships appropriate to their developmental level? I believe the main part of that statement is "peer relationships." If you are seeing a kindergartener who spends all of their free time during recess and lunchtime hanging out with the yard duty lady, they are not interacting appropriately with their peers.

What does this student do during their free playtime at school? If one were to observe a typical group of kindergarten or elementary school children during recess or lunchtime, it would look quite chaotic. However, there is most likely to be some method to the madness. Oftentimes, children are playing in groups of various sizes, maybe running around, or engaging in some type of structured play, such as soccer and handball.

Quite often, kids on the autism spectrum are off by themselves, doing their own thing. However, given the broadness of the spectrum, this can vary greatly. Some children go off by themselves looking for bugs or sticks. Other children on the spectrum could simply be wandering around the periphery of the campus by themselves. Or they could be talking to, or most probably talking at, someone, for instance, lecturing the yard duty adult or their peers about their favorite topic. It is also important to be able to differentiate between the child playing in the same general area as other children and them truly interacting with other children.

Can the child name their friends? Do they play with them at recess and lunchtime? Do the parents know these friends? One of the best questions on the ADOS that is very helpful in truly understanding the nature of a child's peer relationships is asking them about the difference between real friends and the kids they go to school with. There are times when a child on the spectrum thinks everybody in their classroom is their friend and doesn't have a clue as to how to answer this question and what the basis of a true friendship is.

Elementary school

By the start of elementary school, most typical children will be asking for play dates with classmates and children in the neighborhood. Does the child you are evaluating do that? If so, who initiates the interaction? Quite often children on the spectrum can have play dates, but they are initiated by their mother, or maybe by the other child, or the other child's mother.

Dr. Gallo: Does Akiva have any friends?
Parent: No, not really.
Dr. Gallo: What does he do during recess and lunchtime at school?
Parent: He just kind of sits there and keeps to himself. He might run around with the other children from time to time, if he feels like it.
Dr. Gallo: What about at home, does he play with anybody in the neighborhood?
Parent: Now that you mention it, he will play with Josh down the street.
Dr. Gallo: Great, how does that play date come about?
Parent: I will call Josh's mom to see if Josh can come over to play.

Kids on the spectrum often have an "out of sight, out of mind" philosophy regarding interactions with others. It is rather typical for a child to ask for a play date with a friend: "Mom, I'm bored. Could I go over to Emily's house to play?" "Dad, there's nothing to do, can you call Josh's mother to see if he could come over?" Kids on the spectrum are often not the ones to initiate those interactions.

Play dates

One of the many complicating factors you will often encounter when diagnosing individuals on the spectrum is diagnosing an ASD from the myriad of other problems that could be exacerbating or causing these problems. Chapter 12 will be dedicated to this topic. But let's make an attempt to highlight some of the major areas of differentiation, such as cognitive rigidity, social isolation, and a lack of social reciprocity.

Play dates, for individuals regardless of age, are a very good way to gauge the child's social interactions. If the child asks for a play date, then that is a good sign. However, it is important to find out what happens during the child's "typical" play date. For example, just think about what you did as a child or teenager when you got together with a friend. In fact, it may be even easier to think about what you did the last time you got together with a friend. I would imagine that maybe you met at a mutually agreeable restaurant, ate lunch or dinner, and then did something which appealed to both of you, such as seeing a movie you were both interested in, doing some type of activity like shooting pool or simply hung out and talked.

Let's translate your experiences into those typical to the preschool, kindergarten, or elementary school play date. Maybe your friend comes over to your house after school, and the two of you have a snack and then go play together until dinner time or when your friend's parent comes to pick them up. With some modification, I would imagine that would cover most play dates for typical children.

What does the child you are evaluating do during play dates? Does he or she play and interact with the other child? Do they simply want their friend to watch them play their latest video game or talk to them about their intense area of interest for an hour? When the parent goes to check on the children to see how things are going, are the two of them still together and engaged in a cooperative activity? Maybe the friend became bored of watching Ralph play a video game and is now off in another room watching TV, while Ralph continues to play his game?

Does the child interact with peers for short periods of time before there are problems or fights? Sometimes children on the spectrum have a very strict adherence to rules in games (rules which they may have made up themselves), and if the peer does not want to follow those rules, there can be problems.

Is the child currently enrolled, or have they previously been enrolled, in Cub Scouts, Girl Scouts, or Brownies? What does the child typically do during the meetings? Are they paying attention to the pack leader and interacting with their peers? It should be noted that these groups tend to be very popular among parents of children with both ADHD and ASDs, because of their very structured nature.

Has the child taken part in any team sport, such as soccer, baseball, and football? Do they pay attention to what the coach says, or are they "in their own world," doing their own thing, and not interested in what is going on around them? These types of team sports provide children with a great deal of opportunities for social interaction. If there are no children living close by in the neighborhood, this is a good way for children to interact more. When they are taken to either a practice or a match, are they interested in seeing their peers? Do they know the names of their teammates? Do they interact with their peers before and after the game? What about sharing their excitement for what is happening during the game? The answers to all of these questions could provide useful information about the child's social interactions with peers.

A Lack of Spontaneity in Seeking to Share Enjoyment, Interests, or Achievements with Other People

What we are really talking about here is the typical, social human desire to share those things that interest us with others. For example, if you were at the mall with a friend and saw something very exciting, such as a famous movie star or a really cool gadget, you would probably turn to your friend and say, "Andrew, Andrew!!! Look. It's Harrison Ford!" or "Wow, look! I always wanted to get one of these widgets, and now they are on sale. Great!" This typical desire can be lacking in individuals on the spectrum.

Showing and bringing

Young children, typically between the ages of two and six, delight in showing and bringing things to others to look at and to share in their new discoveries.

Dr. Gallo:	When Roni was young, did she show and bring things to you that she liked?
Father:	Yes, all the time. Whenever we went to the mall, she would always grab stuff off of the shelves for us to buy for her.

It is important to note that this is not what this question is asking. In that situation, Roni is not bringing something to her father so that he could share her excitement over the object; she is simply "asking" him to buy that thing for her. There are also times when the parents will answer that their child would bring them a ball or some other toy. However, it is important to determine if the child brought this object to the parent because they wanted to share their excitement with the parent or because they wanted the parent to perform some action with it that they could not by themselves? If my wife brings me a jar of pickles to open for her, then that is not her way of saying, "Honey, I love you and would like you to have a pickle." She simply wants me to perform an action she is not strong enough to do on her own, namely, to open the stuck lid of the jar of pickles.

Let's say the child enjoys playing with balls, which is a pretty typical behavior. Do they bring the balls to the parents or caregivers to play with them? Do they truly want a certain parent or a specific person to play with them, or do they simply want an automaton to throw the ball to them over and over again?

If the patient is a young child, say, of age three or below, will they show the parent something that they find interesting? An inquiry could go something like this.

Dr. Gallo: When you take Stephen to the park, does he show you things that he likes?
Parent: What do you mean?
Dr. Gallo: Well, does he point to the clouds, or a squirrel running by, or another child at the park?
Parent: There are times when he looks up at the clouds. Is that what you mean?
Dr. Gallo: Maybe. When he does that, is he trying to share his excitement of the pretty clouds with you, such as by looking up and/or pointing at the clouds and then looking back at you to see if you are looking? Or is he simply looking up at the clouds and is really not interested if you are looking at the clouds as well?
Parent: I think I see what you mean. No, he simply looks up at the clouds, and that is it.

Even before children can talk, they use gestures and some vocalizations to get their needs met. This talent comes in handy at times. For example, let's say I were taking a trip to France and got very hungry but couldn't speak a word of French. There are things I could do to help get my point across to someone I stopped for help. I could put my fingers and thumb together and put them toward my mouth, back and forth, like I was eating. I could also rub my stomach while doing that. I think it would be a pretty good bet that even if I did not speak French and my new friend did not speak English, I would get my point across. If the child you are evaluating is nonverbal or shows significant language delays, do they compensate for that delay through the use of gestures?

If the answer to that is yes, then that could be a positive sign. If a nonverbal 30-month-old child who is hungry and wants a snack uses sign language or a gesture such as the one I used in my hypothetical trip to France, then that would tell us that the child is trying alterative ways to get their point across. However, if this same toddler simply sat there and cried, without trying to express their needs, then that would be more suggestive of an ASD, as the child may not be making the connection that by communicating with their parents, they can get their needs met.

When it comes to older children, will they show or bring to their parents something they are playing with or something they made at school? When a "typical" child gets a good grade at school, what do they do? Usually, they would show it to a parent. When this older child is at the mall and sees something exciting, will they bring it to the parent's attention, such as by saying, "Wow, Mom! Look what that guy is doing over there!" We need to be quite cautious here to not include objects that are in the individuals' intense areas of interest. For example, if the patient is obsessed with trains (something we are going to be talking about in a later chapter), and that is the only thing they are pointing out to their parents, then that can be a problem, as it could be a sign of an ASD.

Lack of Social or Emotional Reciprocity

The term "reciprocity" comes from the Latin *reciprocus*, meaning "returning the same way" or "alternating." In the context of this book, I use the term to mean this: Does the child you are evaluating do nice things for others? When they were a young child, did they want to feed others or share things spontaneously? When they were two or three years old and their parents would take them for a walk at the park or down the street, would they pick a flower (or a rock, a pinecone, a bug) to give to the parents? If it is an older child who has siblings, have the parents think back to when they were young and were taken to the pediatrician. If they were offered a lollipop, would they ask for one for their sibling? Do they ever ask for anything for another person?

In 1985 Simon Baron-Cohen, Alan Leslie, and Uta Frith published an article titled "Does the Autistic Child Have a Theory of Mind?" in which it was suggested that children with autism have particular difficulties with tasks requiring the child to understand another person's beliefs. These difficulties persist when children are matched for verbal skills (Happe, 1995) and have been seen as a key feature of autism.

Asking about theory of mind is quite important in an autism evaluation because it relates directly to several problem areas commonly found among children on the spectrum. If the child is of grade school age or older, I will often ask the parents if the child knew other family members' likes or dislikes and would want to get something for them at the market or store. For example, if six-year-old Bobby knows that his father likes to eat radishes and reminds his mother of that when they are in the produce aisle at the supermarket, then that would be a good indicator of an awareness of others' preferences. Another example could be a kindergartener taken to the mall by his mother. When the two of them pass by the sporting goods section of a store and the child sees golf clubs, he might tell his mother that Daddy likes to golf and that they should buy him a new club or some golf balls. A child who lacks theory of mind would not have this awareness and could appear rather aloof or uninterested in others' feelings.

It is important to differentiate between a "typical" child wanting to do something nice for someone, such as buying them something that the other person would like, and a very thinly veiled attempt of a child who may be on the spectrum and wants to get something for themselves, such as a five-year-old boy wanting to buy a Transformer toy for Grandma or a bag of chocolate chip cookies for dad. However, it should also be kept in mind that is it not unusual for typical children to engage in this behavior as well.

Chapter 7

The Main Problem Areas of Autism: Language Impairment

As previously mentioned, according to the *DSM-IV-TR*, in order to meet the criteria necessary for a diagnosis of autism, an individual would need to have impairments in three main areas, namely, socialization, communication, and behavior. The *DSM-IV-TR* also states that individuals with autism need to manifest at least one of the problems in this category.

One of my new favorite sayings is "If you have seen one autistic child . . . you've seen one autistic child." The stereotype that an autistic child has unusually delayed language is not necessarily correct. In fact, as is going to be discussed, a language delay is only one of the four possible types of communication impairments needed to fulfill the criteria in this section.

Asperger's versus Autism

It is extremely important to keep in mind from the start of the evaluation that the main distinction between Asperger's disorder and autism is that for a child to have Asperger's disorder, they cannot have a clinically significant general delay in their language development. The *DSM-IV-TR* goes on to define "clinically significant general delay in language" as the use of single words by the age of two and communicative phrases by the age of three. A child with a language delay *cannot* have Asperger's disorder. However, a child with no language delay *could* have Asperger's, autism, or PDD-NOS. When clinicians or other professionals ask me to evaluate a child for Asperger's disorder and then go on to describe problems that include delayed language, it tells me that their understanding of the diagnostic criteria of the ASDs is rather tenuous. Clarity on this point will save a lot of trouble down the road.

Delay in, or Total Lack of, the Development of Spoken Language (Not Accompanied by An Attempt to Compensate through Alternative Modes of Communication Such As Gesture or Mime)

It is important to point out that this delay in the development of spoken language is not accompanied by an attempt to compensate through alternative modes of communication such as gesture or mime. Language development can be an incredibly complicated topic. I remember that one of the very first classes I took in my master's program at Teacher's College, Columbia University, was from an expert in the field of child language development. The textbook for the course was one she had written about the development of language in children from the age of two to the age of three. The book was so detailed and complex that I needed to read it paragraph-by-paragraph, several times, to fully understand what she was trying to tell the reader.

Be that as it may, for the purposes of our evaluations, we only need to keep in mind the specific facts about typical child language development, along with remembering the tremendous variability of "typical." Most children speak their first words by the age of one, and by the age of two they should have a vocabulary of a few hundred words and be able to put at least two words together, such as "mama juice" or "dada up." If the child you see has not reached those milestones, there may be a problem.

Let's take a very blatant example. Assume you are meeting the parents of a three-year-old boy who is not talking at all. The parents tell you that Johnny is their first child and that his only means of communication is to grunt and point. In that situation, you have a clear-cut example of a child with a lack of typical language development. While Johnny definitely needs to be seen by a speech and language pathologist to help him to begin talking, the basic fact that his language development is extremely delayed rules out Asperger's disorder as a possible diagnosis.

A less blatant example of delayed language could be a two- or three-year-old twin who is not speaking because the other twin is speaking for them. Or you could be seeing an 18-month-old who speaks only a few words. In either case, there is a delay but not an incredibly significant one. Living in Los Angeles, with its large multicultural population, I often see children from bilingual households, where one parent speaks one language and the other parent speaks another language. At times, possibly the parents speak one language, while the nanny, the daycare provider, or the grandparent speaks another. There are times when it needs to be determined if the child's language may be delayed because of being exposed to two languages or if that is not a factor at all in their delay.

Another significant aspect that needs to be considered in the child's language development is the possible regression of their language skills. Except if caused by any medical or neurological problem, such as a brain injury or a concussion, a child's language regressing can be a significant sign of autism. This is an instance that is highly suggestive of autism and one that people often think about when autism is mentioned. For example, either language development should proceed on a rather steep upward curve in which the child uses new words often, or the child could possibly plateau for a short period of time and then start picking up new words later.

Having a parent tell you that their two-year-old son only has a 10-word vocabulary may or may not be suggestive of a problem larger than an expressive language delay. However, a parent who tells you that their two-year-old son, who used to have a 200-word vocabulary, has since regressed and now only has a 10-word vocabulary is serious cause for concern. It is very important to note that a regression in the individual's language development when they were very young is not one of the diagnostic criteria for autism. This means a diagnosis of an ASD would not necessarily be ruled out if there were no language regression. However, this is one of those factors that is highly suggestive of autism and should raise some very large diagnostic red flags. It should also be kept in mind that some of those diagnostic red flags could be medically based, such as a tumor, some type of brain injury, or other major medical problem, which should be evaluated by a qualified physician.

Marked Impairment in the Ability to Initiate or Sustain a Conversation Despite Adequate Speech

This is one of those questions that the parent or the caregiver either understands immediately and has a definite reaction to or really does not understand at all. Asperger's disorder has been called "the little professor syndrome," and this area of difficulty is one of the reasons why.

I would imagine that the majority, if not all, of the readers of this book attended colleges or universities where they were enrolled in at least one undergraduate class in a huge lecture hall in which the professor simply stood in the middle and gave their lecture, without the slightest interest in what the students way up in the back were doing. The professor would continue to compare and contrast the works of Skinner and Pavlov or Freud and Jung whether you were paying attention, taking a nap, text messaging someone, or playing Solitaire on your notebook computer. The professor had a lecture to give, and it was not his or her job to care what you were doing. That can often be the case with children on the spectrum.

This area of difficulty relates back to the individual's ability to "read" people, as was talked about in the previous chapter and also connects to the next chapter in regard to intense areas of interest. What we are really talking about here is pragmatics, that is, the study of language used in a social context.

In an elementary school context, good pragmatics could go something like this.

Paul: Hi, Rob! I got a new *Star Wars* toy over the weekend. Look!
Rob: Wow! That's cool. I have the Luke Skywalker one at home.
Paul: Where did you get it? I want one like that.
Rob: My dad got it for me from the mall.
Paul: Boy, you're lucky. I need to ask my parents to get me one too. Do you want to play?
Rob: Yeah! Try and catch me!

The following would be an example of an interaction in which one child did not have good pragmatic skills.

Paul: Hi, Rob! I got a new *Star Wars* toy over the weekend. Look!
Rob: Oh. I really like Pokemon and got a whole bunch of new cards. This one shoots fire and this one . . .
Paul: Yeah, this X-Wing shoots missiles out and it is my favorite . . .
Rob: This one here has a lot of strength, so that it is really tough and hard to kill. I had one like this before, but I can't find it. I think I may have left it in my drawer at home, but I am not sure. Maybe I should look there when I get home. I now have 117 Pokemon cards, but there are still 23 that I am missing. I saw this really neat one at the store the other day . . .
Paul: Yeah, OK, bye.

In this situation, Rob is no longer engaging in any back-and-forth conversation with Paul but is simply talking "at" him. Once Paul realizes that, he leaves to look for a true interaction with another peer.

The following would be an example of poor reciprocal communication skills between a parent and elementary-school-aged child.

Mom: Hi, Honey! How was school today?
Kevin: Fine.
Mom: What did you do today at school?
Kevin: Nothing.
Mom: Did you have fun?
Kevin: Uh [shrugs shoulders].

Mom: Well, while you were at school, I was really busy. I went to the market and
        bought dinner for tonight. We are going to have my favorite, tortilla soup.
        Yummy!
Kevin. Uh.

With this example, we need to keep in mind that just because a child chooses
not to talk with their parents from time to time does not mean that they are
autistic. It is not terribly uncommon for parents and children to have "conversations" like the one listed above. However, if the child does have difficulty in this
area, in addition to numerous other areas common in children with autism, then
we continue to refine the diagnostic picture that appears to point closer towards
an ASD.

Is the child you are evaluating able to sustain reciprocal conversations with
others? You will probably need to provide the parent or the caregiver with several
potential examples of what you are talking about in order for this question to
make sense. There are times when the parent or the caregiver will answer yes to
this question, but it is when you dig deeper that you find out that the individual
is only able to sustain a conversation about their intense area of interest.

Responses to questions in this area need to be interpreted with caution. For
example, let's say you are meeting the parents of a very young child. In that
case, this may not be a valid area to inquire about, as they would be too young
to actually sustain a conversation. However, if the child is a relatively verbal
four-year-old, they should be able to engage in this type of verbal interchange.

Let's look at the response of a mother of this hypothetical four-year-old.

Dr. Gallo: Are you able to chat with Ralph?
Mother: Yes.
Dr. Gallo: Can you give me some examples?
Mother: Well, when I pick him up from preschool, I ask him how his day was
             and he says, "Fine."
Dr. Gallo: OK, but that is not really a conversation. Does he do more than answer
             your questions?
Mother: He tells me that he is hungry and asks me to get him a snack.
Dr. Gallo: OK, but in that situation he is talking to you to get a need met. Does he
             talk to you at other times, or for other reasons, aside from just getting
             his needs met?
Mother: I hadn't really thought about that. No, I don't think so.

This could be considered an inability to sustain a conversation. However, is
that the norm for the child? Maybe when the mother picks him up after preschool,
he is "wiped out" and doesn't feel like talking, but when he wakes up after a nap
or in the morning, he is a very good conversationalist.

What about when you are evaluating preteens with all of the various complicated issues that may go along with that difficult time of life? Here is an example of a hypothetical interview with the parents of a 12-year-old boy.

Dr. Gallo:	Is Akiva able to chat and converse with people?
Parent:	Yes, he will let me know if he wants something and will ask me to buy him a new video game.
Dr. Gallo:	But that sounds more like he talks to you when he wants something. Will he talk to you just for the sake of chatting, either now or when he was younger?
Parent:	Not really, I ask him how school was and he says, "Fine."
Dr. Gallo:	Will he ever ask you how your day was?
Parent:	[laughs] No.
Dr. Gallo:	Does he call people on the phone to talk to them?
Parent:	No, he doesn't even want to answer the phone. He makes me get it.
	[So far, we are getting a relatively clear picture of a preteen who is not very talkative, but we need to determine if he has always been that way or if it is a newer personality trait.]
Dr. Gallo:	When he was a little boy, around the time he was in kindergarten, and the family would sit down for dinner, would he talk about his day or about anything at all?
Parent:	No, he would answer whatever question we asked of him, but he would typically give just a one-word answer.
Dr. Gallo:	Has Akiva's level of verbal interaction, his amount of chatting with you, changed as he has gotten older? I mean is he more talkative now than he was in the past, less talkative now than he was in the past, or about the same?
Parent:	The same.

Now we know that age really has not played a tremendous role in Akiva's poor pragmatics, as the parent has noted that it has always been an area of difficulty for him.

Stereotyped and Repetitive Use of Language or Idiosyncratic Language

The American Heritage Dictionary of the English Language defines "stereotyped" as "lacking originality, creativity, or individuality" and "idiosyncratic" as "a structural or behavioral characteristic peculiar to an individual or group." This area of difficulty for individuals on the autism spectrum is quite broad, and there are several different ways in which these behaviors can manifest themselves.

"Flipping" Pronouns, or Pronomal Reversal

Does the child use pronouns the same way other children their age do? For example, if a typical two-year-old boy wanted to tell you he was hungry, he might say something like "I hungry" or simply "Hungry." Those are pretty standard ways of getting their point across. However, if the child were to say, "Andrew's hungry" or "You're hungry," then that would not be typical.

Just recently, I administered an ADOS to a four-year-old boy who was previously diagnosed with autism by a colleague but was then diagnosed with PDD-NOS by the Regional Center. The parents were requesting the ADOS for additional information to help to clarify the diagnosis. During the 40-minute administration, this child displayed a great deal of pronomal difficulties. For several minutes he played with a balloon and repeatedly said, "We blow, we blow," referring to himself trying to blow up the balloon. He would also refer to himself by his first name and say, "Bobbie balloon, Bobbie balloon," instead of saying, "My balloon." In addition to these pronoun issues, the ADOS was very helpful in identifying several problem areas and truly solidifying his previous diagnosis of autism.

Echolalia

There is a normal part of language development when children are learning to speak, around the age of 18 months, in which they echo or repeat words or phrases other people say. This phase is typically quite brief and is not a cause for concern. However, if the echoing lasts for a prolonged period of time, such as more than a few months, then it would need to be looked into further.

There are two different ways in which echolalia can manifest itself, namely, immediate or delayed echolalia. Each of these two can range in severity. Let's discuss immediate echolalia first.

When a child, or adult, engages in immediate echolalia, they repeat the words others have said, right after they hear them. For example, a mother might say to her daughter, "Valerie, what are you doing?" Valerie could then echo back either the entire sentence, "Valerie, what are you doing?" or the final several words of the sentence, "What are you doing?" Immediate echolalia is typically easier for the parents to notice, as it happens right after they speak to their child.

Dr. Gallo's Pearl of Wisdom: There are times when children echo back not only the words or sentences another person says but also the exact tone, cadence, rate, and rhythm in which they were said. This can be a pretty clear red flag of an ASD.

Echoing behavior starts rather early in the child's development and needs to be differentiated from (1) repeating what was said to them because they are thinking about the answer or (2) repeating it because they are trying to annoy the other person by repeating back what has just been said. In the first instance, it is possible that the individual is attempting to process what they have heard. For example, if I were asked, "What did you have for dinner last night?" I may need to think for a moment and might even ask myself out loud, "What *did* I have for dinner last night?" However, by doing so, I changed the pronoun used from "you" to "I," in addition to changing the tone of the question by putting more emphasis on the word "did." Therefore, I was not echoing what was said to me. An individual who repeats what was just said to them in order to be difficult or funny may do so with a smile on their face, or there would be some other type of indication telling you that they are trying to be obstinate. For the child with ASD, the echoing would be an exact replica of what has been said, but no reply would be stated or implied, leaving the other person wondering if they have understood the question.

Delayed echolalia, on the other hand, can be more difficult for a parent or a caregiver to notice. There may be times in which a parent will ask the child a question, "Emily, how was school today?" and Emily will not answer right away but may echo that question several times over the next 10, 20, or even 60 minutes. There have been several times during evaluations in which I have asked the parent a question and then a few minutes later have heard the child repeating that question to themselves while they are playing. When I point out these instances to the parents as examples of delayed echolalia, they are quite surprised and state that they never noticed that or never heard their child do that before. Once again, the individual being evaluated does not need to repeat what was said in its entirety; they will sometimes just repeat the final few words or even the final word.

Repeating or Reciting Lines from Movies and Television Shows

This may also be considered a repetitive use of language, just like delayed echolalia. What we are talking about here is a child who, for no reason, just out of the blue starts repeating lines from a movie, television show, video, and the like when there is no rhyme or reason to do so.

We need to differentiate this potentially diagnostic behavior from the numerous times people, including myself, either sing along with a song or say the lines from a television show or movie while watching it, which could be considered relatively typical behavior. I remember being in middle school when *The Empire Strikes Back* came out. There was a scene in the movie in which Han Solo was going out into the freezing night to save Luke Skywalker from certain death. The people in charge of the animals they were riding on told Han that he would freeze to death before he got too far. Han's reply to that was "Then I'll see you in hell!" For some reason, that statement became very popular among my peers, and whenever a seventh grader said something that annoyed a peer, such as "You can't do that" or "I'm going to tell the teacher what you are doing," the child would often respond with "Then I'll see you in hell!"

In those situations, where the use of a line from the movie is rather silly, there could be some preteen reasoning behind it. Let's say you and your family just finished watching *Ghostbusters* over the weekend. On Monday, something in your home breaks and you need to call somebody to fix it. When your wife asks, "Who are your going to call?" and your immediate response is "Ghostbusters," while that is rather silly, there is some reasoning behind it, as it is in keeping with the context of the movie all of you saw previously.

That is not what we are looking for in this section. We are talking about children who, for no reason, just be walking down the hallway at home and say "Bond, James Bond" or some line from Sponge Bob SquarePants that is totally out of context to the situation.

Let's look at a few examples, such as talking to the parents of a seven-year-old boy.

Dr. Gallo: When Andrew was younger, say around kindergarten age, would he repeat lines from movies or television shows?

Parent: Oh, sure. I remember him watching whatever show he was into at the time, and if he had seen it before, he would repeat what the characters were saying during the show.

Dr. Gallo: Ok, but would he repeat the lines at any other time, aside from when he was watching the show?

Parent: No.

That information presents a very different mental picture from the next answers provided, with the same hypothetical child.

Dr. Gallo: When Andrew was younger, say around kindergarten age, would he repeat lines from movies or television shows?

Parent: Yes, there have been numerous times when he would hang out at home and I would hear him talking. It was only when I started listening closer that I heard him repeating lines from some of his favorite TV shows.

Dr. Gallo: Would he be saying these lines in his play? Was he maybe trying to reenact what he saw in the show?

Parent: No, he has several of the toys of the characters from that show, but at that time, he wasn't playing with any of them. He was just walking around saying those lines.

Dr. Gallo: Were there other times when Andrew would start repeating lines from movies or television shows for no reason?

Parent: Yes, I remember just a few months ago I was driving him home from school and he just started pretending to be Steve from *Blues' Clues*.

Dr. Gallo:	What did he do?
Parent:	He started repeating what Steve had said on the episode he saw the previous week.
Dr. Gallo	Did Andrew try to include you in this play, or was there a reason why he chose that time to begin talking about the show?
Parent:	No, nothing.

This second example is much more consistent with a child engaging in linguistic behaviors suggestive of an ASD.

Having a Very Literal and Concrete Use of Language

Keeping in mind that no two individuals on the autism spectrum are alike, the majority of them have a very concrete and literal interpretation of language. When I was in graduate school, my fellow classmates and I learned about Kohlberg's stages of moral development. The story, which has many revisions, goes something like this: There was a woman in a small village who was dying, and the only person who could help her was the village pharmacist who had the medicine she needed. However, he charged an unreasonable amount of money for the medicine, and the woman was unable to afford it. Without the medicine she would die; so she broke into the pharmacy and stole it. Was her action acceptable or not? That is an example of a higher-order thought process of a situation that is not black and white.

An individual who is a black-and-white thinker could say that the woman was wrong because stealing is wrong. Period. End of story. The fact that she would have died without the medicine and the pharmacist was being a bad guy by inflating the price so much is beside the point. Stealing is wrong!

This type of concrete thinking can show up with individuals on the spectrum in several different ways. For example, I like to make up names of hypothetical people in my evaluations, such as Ralph. Let's say I were talking with the mother of a five-year-old boy who was brought in for an evaluation and I asked how her son interacts with others. I might say something like "Let's say your son is playing on the playground at school and another boy, Ralph, walks up and wants to play with him." The mother most probably realizes "Ralph" is just a name I made up to represent any random child at school and would be able to move beyond the ambiguity. However, this would be the point at which the child on the spectrum, with a very literal way of looking at the world, would chime in and say, "I don't know anybody named Ralph," and would then not be able to get past that.

There can also be times when questions are asked of the parents to which general answers are acceptable, such as "When does Leah typically go to bed?" While the parent may give a general answer, such as "around 7:30," the child who cannot tolerate the ambiguity would state, "No, Mom, I go to bed at 7:35."

Other examples can include not understanding what is said beyond the literal nature of the words coming out of one's mouth. For instance, several years ago, my colleague Sue met the parents of an autistic child. The mother related an incident in which her eight-year-old autistic son came home from school and talked with his older sister. The sister asked him what he did in school that day, and the brother said he took a test. She then asked the very logical question, "Oh, what was your test on?" The brother got an upset look in his eyes, crossed his arms across his chest, and said, "On paper, stupid!"

Needless to say, the brother's very concrete and literal interpretation of his sister's question was not what she had intended. Clearly, the sister's question meant "What subject did your test cover?" not "What type of material was your test written on?" Just imagine an autistic individual's interpretation of the statements "It's raining cats and dogs out there," "Hop in the shower," or "Get the lead out."

As a more personal example of literal and concrete usage of language, a few years ago, I was lying in bed watching TV with the lights on. When my wife came back to the bedroom, I asked her to "hit the lights." Being in a playful mood, my wife did just what I had asked her to do; she literally hit the light switch. I thanked her for doing what I had asked and then requested her to "please turn off the light," which she did with a big smile on her face.

Does the individual understand sarcasm, proverbs, idioms, and the like? This is a common area of deficit for children on the spectrum. If a peer walked up to them and made some type of sarcastic comment about liking their shirt or their shoes, would the child understand that they were being made fun of? This is one of those complex areas for individuals on the spectrum because of the fact that we are talking about their ability to not only understand sarcasm but also be able to read the meaning of the other person's body language and tone of voice while they are saying it. With sarcasm, it is typically not what is being said but the manner in which it is said. The inability to decipher this information in the majority of people on the spectrum often leaves them open to being set up by their peers, and they will often get into trouble, without knowing why or even how it happened.

Once children enter middle school, this area of difficulty may become a major problem. Being a big fan of animal documentaries, I have noticed that lions in Africa can be used as a very good metaphor for not-very-nice children in school, especially middle school. While hunting the wildebeests and gazelles on the savannah, the lions never choose to target the strong bull wildebeests or the very healthy gazelles. They know that a much easier target would be the baby gazelle at the back or the old wildebeest with the broken leg. Kids can be like this as well. They tend to have a sense that something is different with kids on the spectrum, something that makes them easier to pick on and bully.

The kids on the spectrum, who can't read body language, don't understand sarcasm, and would not think that their peers would intentionally get them in trouble, tend to be set up by others. I have heard several examples of children getting in trouble, even being expelled from school, because they did something their peers wanted them to do, such as exposing themselves to other students, making sexually inappropriate comments to peers, or even stealing from their teachers because their peers told them that the teacher would think it was funny.

Having a Robotic or Monotone Voice

I have heard comparisons made to the *Star Trek* characters Mr. Spock and Commander Data to exemplify a robotic or monotone voice. Does the patient display various and appropriate tones of voice when he or she is expected to? If they are happy, sad, scared, or in pain, does the tone of their voice change to match that emotion? Or are they relatively deadpan and it is often quite difficult to tell how they are feeling? Does their face or the tone of their voice change to reflect their emotions? Some parents have told me that their child tends to always appear happy, even when happy is not the appropriate emotion at that time, such as during the terrorist attacks on 9/11. We would expect most neurotypical individuals who have seen something exciting or just fallen down and got hurt to have a significantly different tone of voice than someone who is reading an entry from the dictionary.

The Little Professor Syndrome

This topic was briefly discussed in a previous section and will be expanded upon here, as it plays an important role in appropriately evaluating an individual for an ASD. It is important to note that almost everybody has a hobby or pastime they are passionate about, and this is perfectly normal. However, most neurotypical people know the time and place in which to have in-depth conversations about their unique interests. If we were to take a man, for example, who has a passion for salt-water fish tanks, it would make perfect sense for him to have in-depth and lengthy conversations with other people at the fish store, who share that interest.

By the same token, this individual should also be aware of the fact that his girlfriend does not share the same interest. When he starts to talk about improving the flow rate of his protein skimmer in the refugium and she starts to look at her watch and yawn, he needs to change the subject. This is not always the case with the people on the spectrum.

Does the person you are meeting talk at (instead of with) others? Are they able to shift their conversation from one topic to another? If you are evaluating a child, do they know significantly more than someone their age should about a certain topic? There is nothing atypical about a child who knows that this dinosaur is a T-Rex and that one is a triceratops, or that this train car is an engine and that one is a caboose. However, when the child's depth and breadth of knowledge about a subject is significantly more than would be expected of a person their age and they start talking at you about this information, we could have another sign of an ASD.

The following is an interview with the mother of an eight-year-old boy.

Dr. Gallo: Is there anything Mordachi is really into and talks a great deal about?
Mother: Well, he really likes his superheroes.
Dr. Gallo: Does he seem to know significantly more about superheroes than other children his age?
Mother: Oh, sure. He is always telling me about the radioactive spider that bit Spiderman and about Batman and all of the bad guys in the Batman cartoon.
Dr. Gallo: What about if you are tired of talking about superheroes and ask him about something else, such as how his day was or what he would like for dinner?
Mother: It is usually very difficult to redirect him when he is talking about superheroes. There are times when I am tired and not even really paying attention because I have heard all of this hundreds of times before, but he doesn't seem to notice. He just keeps talking.

That general presentation would fit the bill for the child being a little professor.

Let's look at a conversation with the same eight-year-old boy in the middle of the interview, after he has had time to acclimate to the office and play with the action figure toys he brought with him to the evaluation.

Dr. Gallo: Wow! That is a cool guy you've got there. Who is that?
Mordachi: It's Batman. His real name is Bruce Wayne. He's a good guy, and he goes around fighting crime in Gotham City.
Dr. Gallo: Neat! I remember that when I was your age, I played with my GI Joe action figure. Do you have any of those?
Mordachi: No, and look. Batman has his cool car in the bat cave that is under Wayne Manor. Did you know that Michael Keaton played batman in the first two movies, but then Val Kilmer and George Clooney played

batman in the next two movies? I really like the new Batman movie, it was really good.

Dr. Gallo: Yes, I liked it too. Are you looking forward to seeing the new Harry Potter movie?

Mordachi: No.

[The child then goes into 5–10 minutes of in-depth Batman information, never asking me a single question or even noticing that I am not interested in talking about Batman.]

Becoming Stuck on Topics, Regardless of the Conversation Occurring around Them

Sometimes either the individual's anxiety or strict adherence to routines (even routines in their minds and known only to them) gets in the way of their ability to shift gears and switch topics.

Conversations between people or groups of people should be a fluid undertaking, kind of like a river. The conversation should be able to twist and turn in whichever direction people want it to. However, some people on the spectrum may have tremendous difficulty with that. Is the child able to switch gears in conversations? If you talk with them about topic A and then switch to topic B, are they able to follow you, or do they continue to come back to A?

An example of this could be a parent having a conversation with their child about something that interests the child, such as Thomas the Train. After a few minutes the parent moves the conversation along to what they need to do when they get home after school or the plans they have over the weekend. However, the child cannot shift gears and continues to talk about Thomas the Train, even after being told by mom that she is done talking about that.

I have been told about instances in which a parent or another adult is talking with an autistic child about that child's intense area of interest. If the child's monologue is interrupted with a question or comment, the child has to go right back to the beginning of the monologue and cannot "pick up from where they left off."

Lack of Varied, Spontaneous Make-Believe Play or Social Imitative Play Appropriate to Developmental Level

In order to have a clear grasp of what we need to look for in terms of play with a child who may be on the spectrum, we need to review the development of play skills in typically developing children. Here are some of the more common play milestones: By 18 months, children should engage in simple pretend play, such as feeding a doll or stuffed animal. Typically, up until the age of two, children mainly engage in solitary play. By the age of two, they should engage in pretend play with others that has more than one action, like feeding the doll and then putting the doll to sleep. They should also enjoy being next to children of the same age and show an interest in playing with them, perhaps giving a toy to another child. Between the ages of two and three is also the time when typically developing children engage in parallel play, which is playing next to another child, doing the same thing they are doing, but not playing with them. By the age of three, a child should enjoy pretending to play different characters with you or talking with dolls or action figures. Additionally, they should enjoy playing with children of the same age, perhaps showing and telling another child about a favorite toy.

It is also important to differentiate functional play from creative or imaginative play. If a child is taking a toy, such as a car, and rolling it along the carpet, he is engaging in functional play with the toy. The function a car serves is to move; therefore, the function of a toy car is also to move. If he tells you that the car is driving to school or is in the Indy 500, he is now being creative and using his imagination.

A child who flies his toy plane around the house is also engaging in functional play. However, if that child tells you that he is flying his plane to the moon or that he is a famous fighter pilot who is going to shoot down the bad guys, he is now engaging in creative and imitative play.

If you are meeting a young child, you need to ask what they play with and how they play with it. If you are meeting an older child, you need to ask the parent or the caregiver how the individual used to play when they were younger. Once again, we need to focus around preschool and kindergarten time. Here is an example of a "typical" response by a parent when asked about play.

Examiner: When Josh was a little boy, around 2 or 3 years old, what would he
            play with and how would he play with it?
Mother: Well, he liked to play with cars and blocks.
Examiner: Did he line them up?
Mother: No.
Examiner: OK, let's go on to something else.

That line of questioning leaves a tremendous amount to be desired and basically tells us nothing. Let's attempt that again with some additional background information.

Dr. Gallo: When Josh was a little boy, around 2 or 3 years old, what would he
             play with and how would he play with it?
Mother: Well, he liked to play with cars and blocks.

Dr. Gallo: What would he be doing with the cars and blocks?

Mother: I don't know. He just basically played with them.

Dr. Gallo: Would he stack them up, line them up, make a story out of what he was doing?

Mother: I don't think so.

Dr. Gallo: Did he ever want to include you in his play? [This question relates to the earlier section on socialization and gives additional information about the patient's social interactions with others.]

Mother: No.

Dr. Gallo: Was there any creativity or imagination in his play?

Mother: Well, he would roll the cars back and forth and stare at the wheels going around. [We are going to talk more about this in the upcoming chapter on behavior.]

Dr. Gallo: Did he make a story out of his play? Would he say that his car is broken and has to go to the garage to get fixed or that his action figure is going to the market to get groceries? Anything like that?

Mother: I don't think so.

Dr. Gallo: Did he ever play dress up and pretend to be a superhero or a villain, such as Superman or Darth Vader?

Mother: No.

Dr. Gallo: When he got a little older, would he play with action figures and pretend he was doing things with them such as storming the beach or flying his ship around the galaxy?

Mother: No.

With those type of intensive questions, I would be much more confident that I truly got to the heart of the matter, knowing that the mother and I were on the same page in terms of understanding what I was asking.

If the child being evaluated has any siblings, do the parents note any differences between how the two children play? If the child has a sibling who is of preschool age or older, I like to ask if the sibling plays with stuffed animals, action figures, or toys in a creative manner. This helps to get the parents thinking about how their children differ in terms of play.

Dr. Gallo: Do you have any other children, or is Roni an only child?

Parents: No, she has two younger sisters.

Dr. Gallo: If you were to compare how Roni played with toys when she was in preschool to how her sisters played at the same age, was there any difference?

Parents: Oh, sure, Roni liked to play with Barbie dolls, and her sisters liked stuffed animals better. [That is not what we are inquiring about here. I need to rephrase my question.]

Dr. Gallo: Ok, but if we thought about Roni when she was a preschooler and then compared her play with that of her sisters when they were preschoolers, did they play with their favorite toys in a rather creative and imaginative way, such as pretending to feed them, pretending that they were the teachers and their dolls or stuffed animals were the students? Things like that?

Parents: No, her sisters did much more of that than Roni did. She typically would just carry her doll around with her and not do anything imaginative like that.

If there are multiple children in the family and none of them engaged in creative or imaginative play when they were younger, this is something that should be kept in mind and would suggest against a diagnosis of an ASD.

If the child is engaging in some creative and imaginative play with others, who is initiating the play? A child who actively seeks out peers to play with in a creative and imitative manner is quite different from a child who just does what others are doing.

Children on the spectrum tend to engage mainly in physical, running-around play such as tag. There is little, if any, creativity or imagination required for playing tag. It could also be helpful to find out if the child is the leader who initiates the game or if he simply watches other children running around and wants to run as well. The child initiating the interaction with peers is a positive, prosocial finding that also needs to be taken into consideration.

Chapter 8

The Main Problem Areas of Autism: Behavioral Concerns

The possible impairments in individuals who are on the autism spectrum can be quite noticeable and therefore some of the most obvious to those without a solid grasp of the spectrum. There are four main types of difficulties, which we will discuss here.

Encompassing Preoccupations with One or More Stereotypical and Restricted Patterns of Interests That Is Abnormal either in Intensity or Focus

We all have hobbies and interests that we can become quite passionate about, but that is not what we are talking about in this section. As noted earlier, when we talked about "little professors," there is nothing wrong with a child, a teen, or an adult being passionately interested in trains, dinosaurs, astronomy, and the like. In fact, it is rather likely that today's astronomers and paleontologists were yesterday's children who were quite enthralled with those subjects. However, the main question we have to ask ourselves here is this: does the individual I am evaluating have an intense, "encompassing preoccupation" with something? Let's look at a couple of theoretical examples.

It could be perfectly normal for a man in his thirties (such as myself) to like *The Lord of the Rings* and to have seen all the three movies a few times. This is quite different from another 30-something-year-old who watches all three movies as many times as possible, has read all of the books numerous times, and knows even the minutest details of the movies as well as the books. He would also be quite happy to tell you about the trilogy, whether you want him to or not, for really long periods of time.

How about a young child who likes Thomas the Train? A child playing with his toy train and really enjoying it, in addition to several other toys, is quite different from a child who is obsessed with Thomas, can only play with Thomas, will only talk about Thomas, and only wants to watch Thomas cartoons.

We need to keep in mind the distinction between really liking something and being obsessed with that object. In Chapter 12, more information will be presented in regard to differentiating between true obsessive-compulsive disorder (OCD) and ASDs.

Let's take the example of an examiner talking to the mother of a four-year-old boy.

Examiner:　Does Johnny have an intense preoccupation with anything?
Mother:　　He really loves Thomas the Train.
Examiner:　That could be a sign of autism. Let's move on to my next question.

Without additional information, the child's interest in Thomas the Train, which could be a sign of the typical behavior of a child, may be interpreted as a sign of autism. Let's revisit that question.

Dr. Gallo:　Does Johnny have an intense preoccupation with anything?
Mother:　　He really loves Thomas the Train.
Dr. Gallo:　How so?
Mother:　　Well, he spends a lot of his time playing with it.
Dr. Gallo:　Does he play with anything else?
Mother:　　Yes, he also likes his action figures.
Dr. Gallo:　When he plays with Thomas the Train, what does he do with the action figures?
Mother:　　He talks about how Thomas is taking a load of lumber over the hill where he will meet his friends or how he is struggling to get up over a mountain.

　　　　　　(These could be examples of creative and imaginative play, which would be a positive, age-appropriate sign, or Johnny could simply be reenacting what he has seen on the cartoon, which may or may not be an ASD trait. We need to keep inquiring.)

Dr. Gallo:　Is what he is doing just a reenactment of what he saw on the Thomas the Train videos, or is it something he made up on his own?
Mother:　　I don't remember seeing that exact scenario on the video, so I think he made it up himself.
Dr. Gallo:　Does he carry his Thomas the Train toy with him everywhere he goes?
Mother:　　No.

| Dr. Gallo: | So if you went out somewhere for a few hours to run errands and he forgot to bring his train with him, what kind of reaction would he have? |
| Mother: | It really would not be a problem. He might say he forgot it, and I would tell him that it is not a big deal, that he can play with it again when he gets home, and then he would be fine and not bring it up anymore. |

This information would suggest that while Johnny really likes Thomas the Train, he does not appear to have an "encompassing preoccupation" with it. This next example is a more cut-and-dried case of a child who would definitely meet this diagnostic criterion.

Dr. Gallo:	Is Ralph really, really into anything or knows significantly more about something than most typical four-year-old boys do?
Parent:	Yes, he is obsessed with vacuum cleaners.
Dr. Gallo:	How so?
Parent:	He loves it when we vacuum and will watch, jump up and down, and flap his hands when my wife or I vacuum. When we go to the mall, he doesn't want to go to the Disney Store to look around; he wants us to take him to Sears to look at the vacuum cleaners. He can spend hours looking at vacuum cleaners. I will usually give him 5–10 minutes to look at them, before I tell him that it is time to go. Of course, when I do that, he has a huge fit, and I usually have to carry him out of the mall while he kicks and screams.

Apparently Inflexible Adherence to Specific, Nonfunctional Routines or Rituals

This can often be a difficult question for parents to answer, given the fact that not many of us like change. Care needs to be taken to ask very specific questions and to be able to "cull out" the information the parents may provide that is not germane to this topic. Let's look at an example of this with the mother of a four-year-old boy.

| Examiner: | How does Sam deal with changes to his routine? |
| Mother: | He hates it. When I tell him that he needs to stop watching television and get ready to go to bed he argues. He also gets upset if I ask him to do something he doesn't want to do. |

How many four-year-old children are there who would be happy turning off the television and going to bed? Or, for that matter, how many of us are happy to be told we need to stop doing something we enjoy to go do something we don't enjoy? Once again, that is not really what the question is asking.

Dr. Gallo:	How does Sam deal with changes to his routine?
Mother:	He hates it. When I tell him that he needs to stop watching television and get ready to go to bed he argues. He also gets upset if I ask him to do something that he doesn't want to do.
Dr. Gallo:	I guess I can't blame him. However, are there certain "rituals" that Sam has or things that he has to do in a certain way over and over again?
Mother:	I'm not sure I understand your question.
Dr. Gallo:	Well, when it is time for Sam to go to bed, does he have a certain routine or order in which he does things? For example, at bedtime, does he have to first get his pajamas on, then brush his teeth, then go to the bathroom, and then have you read a book to him?
Mother:	No.
Dr. Gallo:	So if the family comes home a little late one night from dinner or some outing, and it is past Sam's bedtime, he would be fine if you switched the order of things around?
Mother:	Yes, that is not a problem for him.
Dr. Gallo:	Great! How about if you moved something in the house, like a picture frame or some furniture? Would Sam get really upset?
Mother:	No, that is really not a problem for him.
Dr. Gallo:	What about driving him to school a different way? Or let's say that the two of you have a plan after school that you will go to the bank, then the dry cleaners, and then the market, but then you tell him that you forgot you have to stop by the florist to pick something up? Will that change be a real problem for Sam?
Mother:	No, he is pretty flexible about things like that.

If you are seeing a child for an evaluation, you may want to obtain information about your patient from other sources, such as teachers, grandparents, family friends, pediatricians, and therapists, as has already been mentioned. You will need to get the parent's permission to do so, of course. You will want to ask if the child has fits or temper tantrums. If so, what is it that sets them off? As previously mentioned, most people, especially children, do not like change, but simply not liking something or not being enthusiastic about something is very different from having severe temper tantrums if things are changed or modified. Does the child need to do things in a certain order or in a certain way to prevent a meltdown? It is this criterion of having significant difficulty coping with change that is the most likely reason why so many children who come in for evaluations have previous diagnoses of OCD. In Chapter 12, the factors that differentiate OCD from what we are talking about here will be discussed in greater detail.

Stereotypical and Repetitive Motor Mannerisms

Behaviors such as finger or hand flapping or twisting, rocking, and head banging are "classic" signs of autism. It is often these signs that the less-experienced evaluators and lay people hone in on as the main criteria. With all of the diagnostic criteria, it needs to be kept in mind that the child or the individual does not need to display every sign and symptom with great severity in order to qualify for a diagnosis. As may be remembered from Chapter 5, an individual only needs to have "at least one" of these behavioral issues.

These types of motor mannerisms are considered "self-stims." The individual engages in these behaviors either to rev themselves up, because they are under-stimulated or bored, or when they are overstimulated and need to find a way to calm themselves down.

Does the child have any type of unusual movements? Do they rock back and forth? Did they bang their head when they were little, or do they currently flap their hands? It is not atypical for children to flap or move their hands when excited. However, what we are really looking at here is if these behaviors are self-stims? If the child flaps their hands, when do they do so, and for how long? Can they be redirected? Do they look at their hands when they are flapping? Are there any other types of unusual behaviors that the child engages in? Do they have a history of rocking back and forth, pacing, or banging their head? One of the adolescent psychiatrists I know, Dr. Parrish, once had a patient who would lick his shoulder when stressed.

In some of the more "classic" cases I have been involved with, the children sit in their seats and rock back and forth. However, this is quite rare, and I have probably only seen a few dozen children engage in this behavior during my 1,500 evaluations. More often, the children will become excited about something and either jump up and down and flap their hands or simply flap their hands up and down at the wrists.

You will also want to ask if the child walks on his toes, paces back and forth often, or walks in circles. A child walking on their tip toes is one of those interesting issues that would meet the diagnostic criteria here as a stereotypical or repetitive mannerism.

Sometimes an autistic child's intense anxiety will manifest itself through what could appear to be compulsive behaviors. I recently met a 12-year-old girl and her parents. During our time together, she sat in the chair and appeared to be listening. However, when the parents started talking about their concerns for their daughter, she began rocking forward, straightening her socks, touching her legs, rocking backward, and straightening her hair. This behavior increased to several times a minute, until the parents stopped talking about this anxiety-provoking topic. At that point, the behavior stopped for a few minutes, until the parents brought up the next topic, which again made her anxious.

A child who wanders around aimlessly and flaps his hands often (or walks on his toes all the time, or spins around frequently) would have a much higher probability of being diagnosed with autism than a child who only rocks when playing video games. It is important to keep all of this information in context. Meeting a teenager who is engaging in some self-stim behaviors, such as pacing back and forth occasionally, but has friends and interacts well with others would not provide you with enough criteria to make a diagnosis.

Persistent Preoccupation with Parts of Objects

Another of the "classic" signs of autism is found in this category – a fascination with spinning objects, such as wheels on cars, plates, and fans. Is the child more interested in parts or pieces of objects or toys than the toy as a whole? As you could imagine, it is not typical for people to spend exorbitant amounts of time watching fans rotate or making things spin. There are several other traits that can be included in this section.

Does the individual you are meeting have a history of being "really into" certain things? The typical objects I ask about include pieces of lint, pieces of string, and running water, along with opening and closing the doors or cabinets, turning light switches off and on, spinning objects, and so on. We are not talking here about a child who turns the lights off and on a few times while looking at the parents and smiling, but someone who could be in a room for a prolonged period of time, flipping the switches off and on and being perfectly happy doing so.

One very helpful way that I have found to obtain this information is though the behavioral observations of the individual, typically children, during the evaluation. A year ago, I met a boy and his mother whom I had seen and diagnosed several years ago, when the boy was of the age of three. Throughout our two hours together, the boy rarely interacted with the adults in the room and paced back and forth holding one of my Star Wars toys very close to his face while moving it back and forth. He never asked his mother to look at anything he was doing, and he would only interact with us to ask a question or to get something he wanted. In this situation, the child appeared to be much more interested in either visually "stimming" on the object, as shown by him rapidly moving it back and forth in front of his face, or possibly focusing on just one specific part of the toy with which he was obsessed.

It is advisable to inquire if the child is more interested in playing with pieces of lint, or pieces of string, or a bottle top, or any piece of trash than he is playing with an actual toy. I think we have all been in those situations in which the baby is more interested in playing with the box the toy came in than the toy itself. That is not what this section is talking about. Can the individual spend an inordinate amount of time playing with or being fascinated by something that is really not a toy? I have been told about children who sit in the bathtub for hours just playing with water or have a collection of small bits of trash that they spend a great deal of time playing with and examining. I met another child who had numerous toys, but instead of playing with them, he would go to the kitchen, take all of the Tupperware out of the cabinets and play with that for hours.

All of the above information in the previous chapters has been focused on assessing children. We are now going to switch gears to focus more upon specific questions to ask when assessing teens and adults for autism spectrum disorders.

Chapter 9

Additional Questions to be Asked when Interviewing Teens

It is now on a weekly basis that I receive referrals to assess teens for ASDs. It is interesting to think that as early as five to ten years ago, this simple fact would be rather unbelievable. How could a child with autism grow up to become a teenager with autism, without anyone, such as parents, professionals, or teachers, knowing that they have autism?

Some people might say that this could be due to higher prevalence rates of autism, a greater awareness of the variability of the disorder, and the use of the label "Asperger's disorder" possibly becoming the "trashcan diagnosis" for anyone who is rather odd or peculiar or does not fit in with the crowd.

The most important factor that needs to always be kept in mind when assessing teens for an ASD is their early childhood history. On the referrals I receive for teens to be evaluated, it may be stated that the boy or the girl does not have friends, stays in their room often, and does not want to talk with parents, among other things. These behaviors in teens are not 100% atypical and do not automatically suggest an ASD. We always need to go back and look at what this asocial and rather isolative teen was like when they were in kindergarten and early elementary school.

The information presented in this chapter is to be used in concert with all of the previously provided information and not in isolation. This information is meant to assist in obtaining a better understanding and diagnostic picture of how the social, linguistic, and behavioral difficulties consistent with autism in childhood could manifest in a teenager.

It must also be kept in mind that autism is a remitting disorder, which means that it gets better with time. This would mean that it is likely for a five-year-old boy whose eye contact is quite poor to grow into a 15-year-old teenager whose eye contact is somewhat better. These skills develop over time, even if no interventions are undertaken. A girl who did not engage in any creative or imaginative play with toys at the age of five, could grow up into an eight or nine-year-old who now plays creatively. If one just focuses on the teen's current level of functioning in the three main problem areas of autism, one is not going to obtain the complete picture.

Social Difficulties

Eye contact

If all teenagers required an evaluation for autism because they did not look at their parents when they were being talked to, we would have years-long waiting lists. It is rather typical human nature to not make eye contact with the people who are upset with us or are yelling at us. Parents who say that their teenage son does not look at them when he comes home at two in the morning on the weekend even though his curfew was midnight are not saying much about eye contact. (However, the fact he was out, hopefully with friends having fun, would be a good prognostic sign against autism.) What about when he was younger? How was his eye contact in elementary school and kindergarten? If his eye contact was good then, but is bad now, then it would not be suggestive of autism.

Just to complicate matters, what if the teen's eye contact is good now, but the parents state that their son's eye contact was very poor in kindergarten and something they had had to work on with him, day in and day out, for years? This young man's appropriate eye contact has become a learned behavior and not something that was natural to him. This information would be suggestive of autism.

Reading nonverbal behavior and body language

This area of difficulty among individuals on the autism spectrum is something that should improve as the person ages. The main factor you want to inquire about is, if it is appropriate now, has it always been that way? If you are seeing a 16-year-old girl for an evaluation who is able to tell if her friends are annoyed with her or that her mother has a headache or that she had a tough day at work just by looking at her body language, is that something that she has always been able to notice, or has that only developed more recently?

Friends

When evaluating teens, a specialist is presented with significantly more social opportunities to inquire about. However, it is very important to keep in mind the "typical" teenage angst that needs to be weeded through. Let's look at an example of an interview with the mother of a 15-year-old boy.

Dr. Gallo: Does Ralph have any friends?
Mother: No, all he does is stay in his room and play video games.

If we stopped here and went on to another question, there would be a number of confounding variables such as being depressed, being on drugs, surfing the Internet all day, or having ADHD, none of which involves ASDs, that could account for why Ralph stays in his room.

Let's try again.

Dr. Gallo: Does Ralph have any friends?
Mother: No, all he does is stay in his room and play video games.
Dr. Gallo: Has he always been that way?
Parent: No, just for the past few years, since he became a teenager. When he was younger, he was always out doing stuff with his friends. In fact, it was hard to get him to come home because he was having so much fun with his friends.
Dr. Gallo: So when he was younger, say, around kindergarten and elementary school, he had friends?
Parent: Oh yes. He was the president of his class in third grade and was very popular in middle school. He also played baseball and was the team captain. He always had friends coming over and often went over to his friends' houses. In fact, there were times when I would not see him much at all because he was always out doing something with a friend.

This additional information provides us with a much different picture of the teen we are evaluating. The difficulty of evaluating someone who is in those often-conflictual teen years, in which they can be moody, oppositional, or asocial, can be overcome by keeping in mind that we are looking at a developmental disorder that must have been present since a very early age. A teenager who has only been moody and isolative for a short period of time paints a very different picture than a teenager who has always behaved in that manner.

What does the teen do on the weekends? Do they go out with others? If so, with whom? Who initiates the interaction? As previously noted, an interaction initiated by the patient could be an appropriate and positive sign, whereas interactions that are always initiated by others could be a sign of a problem. As is not surprising to the parents of "typical" teenagers, they are often on the phone. Does the individual being evaluated talk on the phone with friends?

What we are looking for in a teen with an ASD is either a long history of wanting to have friends, but not knowing how to go about doing so, or a long-standing lack of interest in making friends at all. The former teen would most likely fall into the Asperger's category, while the latter would be more autistic.

A while ago, I met a 17-year-old boy Sam who was reportedly never formally diagnosed with autism. The parents stated that he has always had a great deal of difficulty interacting with peers. One of the primary reasons for this difficulty was Sam's extreme rigidity in regard to rules and fairness. Sam had always assumed the role of policeman at school and would take it upon himself to enforce the teacher's rules. If the teacher told the students to stop talking or to take out their textbooks, Sam would become very upset and scold his peers if they did not do as they were instructed. As you could imagine, this behavior did not endear Sam to his fellow classmates. Then, this mild-mannered young man would become very upset because his peers were mad at him, made fun of him, and called him names. During the time in which I was obtaining Sam's history from his parents, he became very anxious and started rocking back and forth and pacing around the room.

Showing and bringing things that interest them to others

With a teenager, we need to keep in mind that they may become somewhat more reserved and even moody, thereby not being interested in showing things to you. Here is a hypothetical example given by the mother of a 14-year-old boy:

Therapist: Does Carlos show you things that he likes?
Mother: No, he is mainly grumpy and really does not want to have much to do with me, or any family member for that matter.

Without additional information, we don't know enough to be able to come up with a hypothesis as to why Carlos acts this way. Let's try that again.

Dr. Gallo: Does Carlos show you things that he likes?
Mother: No, he is mainly grumpy and really does not want to have much to do with me, or any family member for that matter.
Dr. Gallo: How long has that been going on?
Mother: For quite a while.
Dr. Gallo: Well, if Carlos is of age 14 now, does that mean that 10 years ago when he was four years old and you would take him to the park or the beach, he would not show you things that he thought were neat? Such as a cute puppy, or clouds that looked like objects, or a design he would make in the sand?
Mother: Yes, he would do those things. I remember that he would always want me to watch him do stuff, like going down the slide or building something out of his Legos.

Dr. Gallo: So, when you said this behavior has been going on for quite a while, you mean the past few years? Not when he was in kindergarten or early elementary school?

Mother: No, not back that far. That is what makes me so sad. That he was so different and interactive before, and now he is almost shut off from me.

In order for Carlos to meet the diagnostic criteria for this section, he would need to have a long history of this type of social aloofness, going as far back as age three or four and not just the past few years. While it is possible that he could meet the diagnostic criteria in another section, from the information the mother provided in this example, he does not fit the criteria.

Language Difficulties

As individuals enter adolescence, the interest in the opposite sex develops, and the need to have a good verbal interchange becomes more important. Let's take this hypothetical conversation between two high school juniors:

Bob: So, how are you liking Mr. Smith's Psych class?

Sally: Oh, I think it is pretty good. Who do you have for Psych?

Bob: I got stuck with Mrs. Franklin. She's really strict and gives way too much homework. Nobody likes her. What other classes are you taking?

This type of back and forth conversation is like a verbal tennis match, as one person starts with a topic that the other person listens to and then responds to, which is typically about something directly related to what was being discussed in the conversation. This conversation flows nicely, with each person appearing to be interested in what the other person is talking about. This way, each person feels heard and are, therefore, most probably happy.

Take this scenario as an example of poor pragmatics.

Bob: So, how are you liking Mr. Smith's Psych class?

Sally: Oh, it's fine.

Bob: What other classes are you taking?

Sally: Algebra II.

Bob: Cool, how is that going?

Sally: Fine.

Bob: Oh . . .

It definitely does not sound like this interaction with Sally will be leading anywhere for Bob, such as a date. Sally's lack of reciprocity could mean several things. First, assuming Sally is not on the spectrum and does have a good grasp of pragmatics, she is probably not impressed with or interested in Bob. She is probably not interested in going on a date with him. This situation could be looked at very differently if Sally were on the spectrum and did like Bob but simply did not have a good understanding of how to sustain a back-and-forth conversation.

Let's look at how pragmatics could play a role in the life of a teenager. We need to keep in mind the fact that there may be times when individuals are sullen or moody and simply don't want to talk. This is another reason why one must look back at the child's history while making a diagnosis. Let's say a mother brings her teenage son in for an evaluation because she has heard so much about autism on the news lately and thinks he might have it because he doesn't converse well.

Therapist:	You stated earlier that CJ doesn't talk with you much?
Mother:	No, he only gives me one- or two-word answers whenever I ask him anything.
Therapist:	How long has that been happening?
Mother:	Since he has become a teenager.
Therapist:	So, before that time, you and CJ were able to chat and have nice back-and-forth conversations?
Mother:	Yes, when he was in elementary school, he would always tell me about his day and what he did in school.
Therapist:	Would he also ask you questions about how your day was and what you did while he was in school?
Mother:	Sure, we always had really nice conversations. That is why I am so concerned now.

In this situation, the mother reported that CJ's lack of interest in conversing with her is a relatively new problem and has not been around long enough to qualify as one of the possible symptoms of an ASD. Therefore, additional information would have to be obtained if one were to attempt to find out the underlying reason why he no longer talks as much with his mother.

A teenager who shows difficulties in reciprocal language would most probably manifest this problem in one of two ways. Either they would simply have minimal or no interest in verbal interactions with others aside from getting their needs met, or they would often dominate the conversation and always bring it back to their area of intense interest.

Talking about topics from the middle of a thought

This idiosyncratic trait among individuals on the autism spectrum is one that is seen more with teens and young adults than young children. I am sure there have been times when we have all started talking about something out of "left field." For example, I could be talking with my wife about what we are going to have for dinner and then mention that I really want a new iPod. This is a tangential comment that could be rather confusing. While I know exactly how I got from topic A (dinner) to topic B (new iPod), my wife may not.

A large number of individuals on the autism spectrum lack "theory of mind". They have not developed the insight to recognize that the other person they are talking to may not understand the 90° turn your brain just took to get to a new topic. Theory of mind also comes into play when individuals on the spectrum start talking about topics from the middle of the sentence, assuming that since they understand what they are talking about, others do too. For instance, the parent, the sibling, or the teacher may tell you about how the patient will approach them and just make some random comment such as "23" that does not make any sense to them. The typical response one might have in that situation would be "Huh?" The person would again respond, "23." When they are told, "I have no idea what you are talking about," they might become upset, since they know exactly what they are talking about. Because they know what they mean, you must know as well!

Let's look at a more neurotypical way in which this conversation could have occurred between two individuals (Neurotypical is the standard autism spectrum community word for the average, typical person who is not on the spectrum.)

Bob: Hey, remember yesterday when you asked me about that movie with Jim Carrey?
Sue: Yes?
Bob: I just remembered, it was called *23*.

In that situation Bob realizes that if he just went up to Sue and said "23" as the answer to yesterday's question, she would not have any idea what he is talking about because she is not still thinking about it. However, by providing her with a reminder of the topic, the two of them are now on the same page – and everybody remains happy.

Behavioral Difficulties

When interviewing teens and parents of teens, a very typical and often-heard response is that the teen is obsessed with the television, computer, cell phone, or some type of video game system, such as an X-Box or a PlayStation. It is crucial to be able to differentiate between the individual having a "typical" interest in those things as opposed to obsessed with them. Obtaining additional background information is the key. As could be imagined, if having a teenage girl who is obsessed with talking on the phone or a boy who is obsessed with sports was a sign of autism, we could have a real diagnostic overload.

Let's look at an interview with the father of a 15-year-old boy.

Dr. Gallo:	Does Andrew have any obsessions with anything or is it really, really into something?
Father:	Well, he sure does spend a lot of time on the computer playing that online game, whatever it's called.
Dr. Gallo:	Can you tell me more about his interest in the game?
Father:	He really wants to play it. As soon as he comes home from school, that is all he wants to do. If we let him, I bet he would probably play it all night.
Dr. Gallo:	Do you have Andrew finish his homework before he plays his game?
Father:	I think so. I don't get home from work until dinner time, but I think my wife has him do his homework first.
Dr. Gallo:	When it is time for him to stop playing his game and have dinner, or go do something else, is there a problem?
Father:	He may complain for a little bit, but it is nothing too terrible.
Dr. Gallo:	When Andrew was a little boy, around preschool and kindergarten age, was there anything he was extremely interested in or anything that his world revolved around?
Father:	No.

We always need to look back into the history of the people we are assessing to see if what the parents are concerned about are "typical" interests or something more. A teen who has just developed an "obsession" with something as a teenager, or as a preteen, would probably not meet the criteria we are talking about here.

However, this next teen *would* meet the diagnostic criteria.

Dr. Gallo:	Is there anything David is really into or obsessed with?
Mother:	Yes, he is obsessed with that Pokemon video game and wants to play it all day, every day.
Dr. Gallo:	How long has that been going on?
Mother:	For a couple of years, but before that, he was just as obsessed with Spiderman, and before that it was Star Wars, and before that it was Thomas the Train.
Dr. Gallo:	Do you have any other children?
Mother:	Yes, I have a teenage daughter as well as a 10-year-old son.
Dr. Gallo:	OK. So if we compared David when he was in kindergarten and early elementary school to his siblings when they were that age, was David's interest in those things you mentioned the same as that of your other children?

Mother:	No, not even close. When my other son, Sam, was in kindergarten, he liked to play with army men and Legos, but he was not obsessed with them.
Dr. Gallo:	So, would Sam play with other toys aside from the army men and Legos?
Mother:	Sure, he might play with those for a little while and then get bored and want to play with something else, or he would come ask me if he could go across the street to play with his friend Albert.
Dr. Gallo:	But David was not like that?
Mother:	No, when he was in kindergarten, David was really into Thomas the Train, and that is all he would want to play with, all day.
Dr. Gallo:	Would he want to include you in his play or have you watch what he was doing?
Mother:	Very rarely. Occasionally, I would make some comment about something he was doing that I though was neat, but he would appear kind of annoyed whenever I would interrupt him. So I stopped doing that after a while.

In this situation, while David is obsessed with something now, he also has a prolonged history of obsessions with various objects. By asking the mother to compare David's intense level of interest with that of her other children when all three were young, we are able to assess if what the mother is concerned about is really outside of the norm for other children.

Chapter 10

Additional Questions to be Asked when Interviewing Adults

As noted previously in the chapter about diagnosing adolescents, the information presented here is to be used to supplement the information from the previous four chapters, as that information is crucial in making an appropriate diagnosis.

Socialization Difficulties

Now that you are seeing an adult for an evaluation, you have even more social experiences to draw upon, such as employment history. The job environment is one of the main areas in which adults socialize, and it can provide you with a great deal of diagnostically useful information.

A main question to ask of your adult patient during the evaluation is if they are employed. If so, what do they do? While there is a wide variety here, depending upon how affected they are by their autism, typically adults on the spectrum do not work (or for that matter, work for a long time) in positions where they have a great deal of interaction with the general public. Adults on the spectrum may work the night shift or in a store room, where they don't have to interact much, if at all, with anybody. People on the spectrum typically do not thrive in jobs that require a great deal of interpersonal contact.

Not long ago, I was referred a 50-year-old gentleman, whom I will call Bob, who was concerned he may have Asperger's disorder. Bob thought this because he did not have much luck in relationships and felt he could not show empathy for others' feelings. Bob was referred from his psychiatrist who had diagnosed him with an avoidant personality disorder.

When I first met Bob in the waiting room of the clinic, he made good eye contact with me and shook my hand. When I asked him to tell me about himself, he reported being in the military for several years before being honorably discharged. He then worked for 15 years stocking shelves at various office supply stores throughout the area. He then left that employer to work at his current job, where he has been gainfully employed for the past 12 years. He now works at the front desk of a major corporation where he has to interact with the public as well as with the company employees almost constantly.

I was very curious to delve deeper into his employment history to see if there would be any clues that would support a diagnosis of an ASD. While Bob was in the military, he reported getting along fine with his fellow soldiers and not having any problems. For his first post-military job, Bob was always placed in environments in which he would interact with numerous store employees, from the head manager to the clerks. Once again, no difficulties were noted. When I asked him about the circumstances behind leaving that job, he reported being well liked and simply resigning because he wanted a higher-paying job. At his current job, Bob interacts socially all the time and has reported never having any type of interpersonal conflicts or even having been talked to or counseled by his employer for any type of social or interpersonal difficulties in all that time. In fact, he reported receiving various acclamations from his employer for the good service he provides.

Bob's job history sounds quite good and does not provide evidence that would support a diagnosis of an ASD. Not long ago, I met a young man in his thirties who had a much more "typical" autistic job history. After graduating from high school and dropping out of community college, John worked at a couple of fast food restaurants. When he had to work at the register and interact with the public, he would become very nervous and have great difficulty getting the order right and providing decent customer service. However, when he was allowed to be in the back room or engage in solitary tasks, he was able to perform somewhat better.

After a short period of time, John was fired from several fast food restaurants before finding a job working alone taking care of animals, something he had always enjoyed doing. However, even there, his interpersonal difficulties showed through, and he began having difficulties. The last I heard, John was unemployed because of the stress put on him by working.

Aside from job performance, how does the patient perform at work socially? What do they do during lunchtime or break time? Do they sit in the cafeteria by themselves, or do they have friends whom they eat with? Do they see their friends and coworkers outside of work for a drink or for softball, and billiards, among other things? Do they attend various workplace-related social functions?

As could be imagined, people choose careers, typically, according to what they are best suited for. For example, it would be rather unlikely for a very outgoing and gregarious person to choose to be cooped up in an office with basically no human interaction. However, that type of job may be exactly what an individual on the spectrum is looking for.

Does the adult you meet have a history of work difficulties? Some of the problems we are looking for here could include getting in trouble or having to be talked to by an employer for not socializing well with fellow employees. This was quite evident in my example of John.

If the patient gives you permission to talk to their employer, you would want to ask how they get along with others. Are they social? Do they appear to get along well with coworkers? Have there been any workplace difficulties between the patient and other employees? One example could be a man engaging in what he believes to be social banter or flirting with a female coworker while she views it as sexual harassment. It is important to keep in mind that I am not suggesting that everyone who sexually harasses a coworker has autism, just that if a person never mastered the art of reading nonverbal cues, they would probably not be able to determine if someone was not interested in them.

Dating, Marriage, and Relationships

As could be imagined, adults on the spectrum have the most difficulty in this area. Of the two gentlemen I talked about in the previous section, 30-year-old John has gone on one blind date, which was set up by a coworker, and the woman he went out with was the sister of the coworker. As noted, there was not a second date.

With Bob, he has had a few first dates in his 50 years but no second dates. You would want to determine if the adult is interested in dating. An individual who wants to date and be in a relationship and do nice things for another person can be quite diagnostically different from a more classically autistic individual who is quite isolative and has no interest in making or keeping friends, nor dating.

Why are they having difficulty dating? Are they just shy and do not want to approach others? Have they been making attempts and asking others for dates but have just been turned down? Are they so busy with some type of self-imposed daily ritual or routine that they do not allow themselves any time to date?

If the adult you see for an evaluation is married or has had a significant other for any length of time, then that could be a good sign that they are not on the spectrum. However, it would be foolish of me to make a blanket statement that no one who is married is on the spectrum. In fact, there has even been a few books written about married people on the spectrum, such as *An Asperger Marriage* by Chris Slater-Walker, Gisela Slater-Walker, and Tony Attwood; *The Other Half of Asperger Syndrome: A Guide to an Intimate Relationship with a Partner Who Has Asperger Syndrome* by Maxine C. Aston; and *Alone Together: Making an Asperger Marriage Work* by Katrin Bentley and Tony Attwood.

It could be very helpful to have the partner join the patient for the evaluation. If there are social difficulties in the marriage or relationship, how long have they been occurring? Are these difficulties issues that the patient has always displayed, or are they new?

If the wife says that she thinks her husband has Asperger's because he does not buy her flowers anymore after 15 years of marriage, then the vast majority of us husbands out there could be in trouble. However, if a girlfriend tells you that her boyfriend has never done anything nice for her, has never thought about her feelings, and really cannot chat with her on the phone in the past few years that they have been together, this could warrant additional information gathering.

So as to not be sexist, we need to keep in mind that it is also possible for the women to be the partner on the spectrum here. A few years ago, I met a married mother of two who was concerned she may have Asperger's. She reported never having had friends and not really having much of a life outside of her family, in addition to being very shy in social situations. With additional digging, I was able to uncover some social interactions, but overall, she met the criteria for Asperger's and was quite insightful in her desire to be evaluated.

Language Difficulties

The pragmatics of language are incredibly important at all stages of our lives. When we are adults, pragmatics plays a tremendous role in helping us to secure employment. I often tell the parents of the teens and adults I am working with about why attributes such as good eye contact and pragmatics are so important. I tell these individuals and families that when I was interviewed for my position at Kaiser-Permanente in 2000, the psychologist who interviewed me, Dr. Len Sushinsky, did not ask me incredibly in-depth questions about psychopathology or therapy or psychological assessments, but we simply talked and chatted for about five hours over a two-day period. I have always firmly believed that Dr. Sushinsky felt that I was qualified from looking at my résumé but really wanted to determine if I would fit well, personality-wise, with him and the clinic. I believe the fact that I was able to make appropriate eye contact, be social, and chat with him was truly the key to my employment.

Given the fact that the level of impairment people with autism face improves with time, adults on the spectrum should improve in all areas, including pragmatics, as they age. Here is a hypothetical example of an interview with the mother of an adult patient.

Dr. Gallo: If we go back to when Kevin was in kindergarten or elementary school, did he converse with people?

Mother: A little bit.

Dr. Gallo: What do you mean?

Mother: Well, when a friend of ours or another child would talk to him, Kevin would always talk to them about astronomy, even if that was not what they asked him about.

Dr. Gallo: Can you give me an example?

Mother: It still happens now. When his father or I ask him how his day was, he will usually say, "Fine," and then start talking about Saturn's rings or Jupiter's moons. I don't understand why he can't tell us anything about what his day was like. He can spend an hour looking at the floor and spouting minutiae about the atmosphere and other stuff that nobody even cares about. I can see how people don't want to hang out with him when he doesn't show any interest in what they are talking about and always redirects the conversation back to astronomy.

This "little professor syndrome," which is often a significant component of Asperger's disorder, can become more apparent as an individual gets older. The reason for that is connected to two other areas that we need to look at during an evaluation, namely, the ability to read others and intense areas of interest.

Let's look back at an example of the child who knows a great deal about dinosaurs. When that individual becomes an adult, as a neurotypical, he would probably have developed new, or at least additional, interests to occupy his time. He would also be significantly more adept at reading people's nonverbal behavior and body language. As such, he would be able to deduce when he is boring someone. Here are a couple of examples.

Bob: Hey Ralph. Long time, no see. Anything new?

Ralph: Hi, Bob. Yea, I saw this great IMAX movie about dinosaurs. It was really cool. It talked all about these new theories about what the dinosaurs were like, that some of them had feathers and some were vegetarians. It was pretty cool.

Bob: That sounds good. My girlfriend and I saw a good movie also last week. It was about . . .

Ralph: It was really cool how it used these 3D effects to show what the velociraptors looked like. I didn't know that they had feathers, and I would have thought they would have been bigger.

Bob: Oh, Ok. Great . . .

Ralph: And then it even talked about all of these various mudslides that might have happened in the Jurassic period that could have covered up a bunch of the dinosaurs, and now there is a great new area where paleontologists are looking for a lot of cool new bones.

Bob: (looking at his watch) Yeah, nice talking to you. Bye.

In this example, it is quite obvious that Ralph knows a great deal about dinosaurs. However, he is not truly talking "with" Bob; instead he is simply talking "at" him. He did not appear to notice or care that Bob wanted to talk about a movie he saw with his girlfriend. Here is an example of a more typical interaction.

Bob: Hey Ralph. Long time, no see. Anything new?
Ralph: Hi, Bob. Yea, I saw this great IMAX movie about dinosaurs. It was really cool. It talked all about all of these new theories about what the dinosaurs were like, that some of them had feathers and some were vegetarians. It was pretty cool.
Bob: Ok, my girlfriend and I saw a good movie also last week. It was about World War II and trying to knock out some of the German anti-aircraft guns.
Ralph: Oh, was it good? I was thinking of going to see that with my wife. Do you think we would like it?

In that situation, there is a much more "typical" flow to the conversation, and it is not one-sided. With a little professor, the other person is lectured regardless of their interest in the subject, and all nonverbal attempts to stop the lecture are completely ignored.

The 30-year-old Hispanic woman I spoke about in earlier chapters, whom I had to testify about to support my diagnosis of autism, had a boyfriend whom she was rather obsessed about, but her pragmatics were so poor that he broke up with her. He would call her to say hi and chat, but she would typically only respond with one word, and the boyfriend would usually have to resort to telling her to put her sister on the phone so that he could find out what was new with her.

Behavioral Concerns

When interviewing an adult, all of the above-mentioned information needs to be kept in mind. One should also consider the person's ability to read others (to determine if they are as interested in the topic as he is) and the pragmatics of his language (if the person engages in a dialog with other people about his interest or simply "monologs" at them).

Going back to the 50-year-old man whom I evaluated, toward the beginning of his evaluation, Bob stated he will become locked into schedules and have difficulty deviating from them. I asked Bob about his military and employment history in which schedules or timetables were changed on a frequent basis. He stated that he did not have any difficulty with that. I asked him, "What about if your daily work schedule was planned out so that you would do A, then B, and then C before lunch, and then X, Y, and Z before going home for the day. But then your boss switched all of that around on you. Would you have problems with that?" He stated no. In more than two decades that he had spent at his past two jobs, Bob never had difficulty with being flexible or going with the flow. I asked him if there would be any problem if he had to take his lunch break at a different time than usual or in a different location than usual. He reported that things like that were never a problem for him. This is not a typical finding for adults on the autism spectrum. Typically, an adult with autism either would have a long history of difficulty coping with changes to routines or schedules or would have been working on correcting that and would have had difficulty in the past but not any more.

I asked Bob every question I could think of that related to having problems coping with changes, and he did not endorse any problem. He was never fully able to explain to me what he meant by being "locked into schedules." I think it is important to note that in Bob's example, the information provided on the referral about him, such as his thinking that he has Asperger's, having a lack of empathy for others, having no relationships, and being locked into schedules, sure made it sound like a diagnosis would be a slam dunk. However, by being able to peel back the layers of the onion and trying to fully understand him, it was found that Bob really did not meet the diagnostic criteria after all.

Let's take two examples of an assessment of a 40-year-old, unmarried man who comes in with either a parent or a sibling. Once again, just meeting with the patient himself would typically not provide sufficient information to either make or rule out a diagnosis, as the individual would probably be unable to tell you about himself as a young child or his other areas of difficulty.

Dr. Gallo:	Jim, are there subjects or topics that you are really interested in?
Jim:	Well, I really like fish tanks.
Dr. Gallo:	I think aquariums are really fun. Do you spend a lot of time on it?
Jim:	Yes.
Dr. Gallo:	Is this something you talk about all the time with people, or do you also have other hobbies that you talk about?
Jim:	Oh, I also like to read.
Dr. Gallo:	Mom, when Jim was a little boy, was there anything that he was really into, or fascinated by, or obsessed with?
Jim's mother:	I remember when he was a little boy, he loved to play with his toy cars and build things out of his Legos.
Dr. Gallo:	Were those the only things Jim would play with or talk about at that age?
Jim's mother:	No, I think those were his favorite toys, but he would also play with his sister and play with other toys we had around the house.

Dr. Gallo: So, did Jim's interest in his toy cars and Legos seem pretty similar to his sister's level of interest in her toys when the two of them were little?

Jim's mother: Yes.

In this situation, it would appear that Jim's level of interest in both aquariums and reading at the present time and Legos and cars when he was younger would not qualify as an "encompassing preoccupation." However, that would not be the case in this next example:

Dr. Gallo: Jim, are there subjects or topics that you are really interested in?

Jim: Well, I really like fish tanks. I just picked up a new Maxima clam for my tank, and I was thinking about getting a large refugium to hang on the back. However, the tank is developing an overgrowth of hair algae, and I might need to add some potassium to take care of that. When I was on this Web site last night that talked about ways to control algae, they gave me a lot of good ideas that I hadn't thought about before. I am thinking that maybe I will get a bunch of inverts to control it that way. But then there was this guy on the Web site last night who said that the pump for my protein skimmer was not powerful enough to work well, but he was wrong. I memorized the specs on that pump and wrote him a three-page reply telling him he was wrong!

Dr. Gallo: Wow, Jim. That was a lot of information! Mom, when Jim was a child, did he have other interests that he was as passionate or knew as much about?

Jim's mother: Oh, yes. He was really into insects and bugs and could talk at you about it for hours. As soon as one of my girlfriends or one of his father's coworkers would come over, Jim would go right up to them and tell them all about bugs. He would ask them what their favorite bugs were and all of these various bug facts that I never really understood.

In this example, Jim has a much clearer history that would be consistent with an "encompassing preoccupation" and most probably qualify for the diagnosis.

Several years ago, I attended a dinner party for an autism-related organization in the Los Angeles area. When I was making small talk with an acquaintance, there was another man nearby who came over and started telling me about the various code names that were used in World War II for the beaches of Normandy. Given the fact that my acquaintance and I were not talking about anything remotely related to beaches, codes names, World War II, or France, this is a great example of this gentleman having an encompassing preoccupation with something (WWII in this case), which he will interject into conversations around him, whether or not it flows with the conversation.

Chapter 11

Other Important Factors to Take into Consideration

As can be imagined, it takes more than just answers to the questions given in the previous five chapters to provide the clear picture required to determine if an individual is on the spectrum. In this chapter, additional signs and symptoms will be presented that are not diagnostic criteria listed in the *DSM-IV-TR* but are still quite telling and helpful in determining a diagnosis.

Physical Affection

When the child was younger, such as when they were an infant or a toddler, did they like to be picked up and cuddled? Did they seem to enjoy physical affection? It is important to note the difference between the child hugging the parents when they wanted to hug the parents and when the parents wanted to hug them. Will they only hug parents or others when they want to or at any time? Is the child rather "standoffish"? If they give someone a hug, will it be a two hands around them, rocking, loving hug, or is it more of a stiff-as-a-board, "I really don't want to do this, so here you go, and now leave me alone" hug?

Is the individual, at any age, indiscriminate about who they hug? Do they come and hug you the first time they meet you in your office? Quite often, children on the spectrum do not like to be picked up and held. From an early age they become stiff and rigid when giving a hug. Sometimes, children on the spectrum will only hug one person, such as the mother, and nobody else. There are times when they will only want to hug on their terms, when they are "sensory seeking" but not when someone else wants to hug them. There are also individuals who do not know their own strength and will hug too strongly. Oftentimes, children on the spectrum are not the cuddly type. They tend to prefer to be left alone and do not like physical affection.

With this example of hugging, we need to keep in mind the inconsistency of the spectrum. With all of the information presented above, one could still come across a child on the spectrum who enjoys being hugged and would indiscriminately hug strangers at the supermarket.

Social Interactions in Infancy

There has been a tremendous push in the past few years to make diagnoses of ASDs as early as possible, so that the children can get the services they need to help correct these issues. At such a young age, say, at age two and younger, several of the standard questions that would be asked in cases of an older child do not make as much sense. For example, a two-year-old is not able to read social cues. If they do not engage in interactive play, then that is not a sign of a problem, just typical development. However, there are diagnostic factors that can be looked into further at this young age.

If an infant or young toddler is brought for an evaluation, one would need to ask questions such as the following: When you come into the room where they are, will they track you with their eyes? Do they enjoy interactive social games such as peek-a-boo with their primary caretaker? Many typical children enjoy that interaction and want the other person to repeat them. Children on the spectrum do not have much of a response in those situations.

Does the child wave goodbye, respond when their name is called, or look at the person who is talking to them? These are all factors that need to be taken into consideration. If the young child does not respond in these social situations or to these social overtures, then that could be suggestive of an ASD.

Separation Anxiety

Around seven to eight months, most children have developed some separation anxiety from their primary caretaker. This is typically manifested by the child either crying or attempting to crawl after the adult when that person leaves the room or leaves their line of sight. When the child you are seeing was that age, what was their response? This is one of those situations in which crying and being upset is the norm, and no response is a concern. It also needs to be kept in mind that not having any reaction does not mean that the infant is on the spectrum; it is just something more to think about.

Overly Easy Baby

Going back to the premise that the only thing consistent about children on the autism spectrum is that they are inconsistent, there have been a large proportion of children who have ended up being diagnosed with autism who were very easy babies. They were the types of babies parents loved because they were so laidback and easy-going. When they woke up from their nap in their crib, they did not cry out at all but were totally fine, entertaining themselves for a significant amount of time. As noted in the above section, these could often have been the infants who were not bothered by the mother walking out of the room, as they were most likely busy doing their own thing and didn't notice. This of course does not suggest that infants and children who are overly fussy and hard to soothe are less likely to be on the spectrum, but it is just another tool to be used in a diagnostic evaluation. In fact, knowing if the infant, toddler, or young child was extremely fussy and would often throw a tantrum is also important information that should be obtained.

I saw a three-year-old boy in the past whose grandmother noted he was the "perfect child," as he would stay wherever she put him, even for prolonged periods of time. She recalled an instance in which her husband was in the hospital, and she and her grandson would go visit him for the entire day. The grandmother would place the boy in the stroller or on the floor, and he would simply sit there and not fuss or require any attention for hours at a time. Needless to say, that is not typical child behavior.

Wandering Away

Around the ages of two and three, children start to separate from their parents and strive for more independence. In this stage, the typical child is kind of like a rubber band, which means that they will wander off a short way, feel that they are getting too far away from their parents, and then come back to check in or get a hug. They may then travel somewhat farther away before coming back, but they don't simply continue to wander away. If, for some reason, a typical child does wander away and get lost or separated from their parents, it is usually a traumatic and powerful learning experience for them and something they are not going to do again any time soon.

Wandering off needs to be differentiated from playing and hiding. I would imagine we all know children who get bored while visiting the department store with their parents and hide in the middle of a clothes rack, giggling and waiting for their mother to find them. This is very different from the behavior of the child on the spectrum, who simply wanders away and does not have any feeling of concern or fear about being separated. While the unfortunate parents are having a heart attack and calling the security to lock down the store, Johnny is a few aisles over, having a great time looking at the toys, or ceiling fans, or whatever interests him. By the time this hypothetical child is found, the parents are a wreck and scared out of their minds, while the child does not have any idea what all the fuss is about. Children whose parents do not take their child out in public for fear that they might wander off may be on the spectrum. Of course, this information needs to be considered in the larger context of the evaluation and all of the other information that has been collected.

While the above-mentioned incident could happen with more typically developing children, including children with ADHD, there are some kids on the spectrum who wander away to such an extent that it has a dramatic effect on the family and could even become life threatening. I have met several families that reported having had locks and deadbolts toward the tops of their doors installed because the children would unlock the door and simply wander away. Some of these children were found by neighbors, wandering several houses away without a care in the world.

This can also be a significant problem at school, as some autistic children have been known to wander out of their classroom or to wander off at lunchtime or recess. There was a child I saw whom I diagnosed with autism, but the school district did not agree with me. When the school psychologist went to meet the child to begin her evaluation, he was nowhere to be found. He was not in the classroom or in the yard with his peers, nor in the library, cafeteria, or lunchroom. They simply could not find him. Once everybody got very worked up about where this child could be and all of the horrible things that might have happened to him, someone found him off by himself in some remote part of the school yard, having a grand old time playing with sticks. Needless to say, that experience went a long way toward solidifying a diagnosis of autism with the school district.

Lack of Fear and Stranger Danger

At a young age, infants and toddlers should have a healthy fear of strangers and other entities that could potentially be harmful to them, such as animals, heights, and maybe even some play equipment. A trait that is common among children on the autism spectrum is the lack of fear. Does the child being evaluated appear to recognize danger and take appropriate steps to prevent it? Is the child somewhat of a thrill seeker and simply has no concept of the danger? This could be shown by the child enjoying climbing up on furniture, or a tree, or play equipment and jumping off. It should be noted this lack of fear could also be a sign of impulsivity often associated with ADHD.

As a parent of two children, I believe I have the same fear most parents do, namely, that someone will abduct my child. Luckily, I have great confidence that if a stranger approached my ten-year-old daughter and told her he had some candy for her in his van or had a couple of cute puppies that he would like to show her, she would not go with him. While a child does not have to be on the spectrum to be preyed upon by a perpetrator, children on the spectrum appear to be much more willing to go with a stranger. These children often do not recognize the danger inherent in a situation and can often be an easy victim. You would want to ask the parents if their child shows an appropriate amount of fear in a situation in which it would be expected.

How does the child respond to strangers in general? Do they tend to be overly fearful or to show no fear, or are they somewhere in between? Kids on the spectrum tend to be on one of the two extremes, but we need to keep in mind the inconsistency of the spectrum.

Picky Eating

Having a child who is a picky eater is almost par for the course. We are not talking here about the typical child who only wants to eat their hamburger plain or doesn't want any sauce on their spaghetti. There are times when children on the spectrum can be incredibly picky eaters, such as only wanting to have chicken nuggets from McDonalds and nowhere else or only plain rice at home. Kids on the spectrum could simply refuse to eat for a day or more because you do not have the food they want.

If parents have set rules about eating, such as only making one main dish for the family and not making a special separate dish for the child, most typically developing children soon realize that what is presented is their only choice, and they are likely to eat at least some of it. I have seen children on the spectrum who are such picky eaters that they will only eat specific things, and if those are not provided, even if the store-bought chicken nuggets are disguised to look like McDonald's nuggets, they will go hungry.

Picky eating is also an issue which tends to resolve itself somewhat with age. An eight-year-old child on the spectrum could have the same difficult eating habits as the typical three- or four-year-old. What I typically like to ask the parents here is the impact the child's eating habits are having on the family.

Let's look at two hypothetical examples of picky five-year-olds.

Dr. Gallo:	Is Harry a picky eater?
Mother:	Yes, and it is pretty difficult to feed him.
Dr. Gallo:	How so?
Mother:	He only wants to eat hot dogs, plain hamburgers, or rice. If I make a nice dinner of spaghetti or a baked chicken, he doesn't want to try it. He only wants me to make him a hot dog or a burger.
Dr. Gallo:	If the family were at the mall on the weekend and everybody wanted to have lunch, would it be a problem for Harry to find something to eat?
Mother:	No, we could always go to a restaurant, and he could get a hot dog or hamburger. It really is not a problem.
Dr. Gallo:	What if the hamburger and hot dog restaurant were not open yet or if there were no such place where you were?
Mother:	He would find something to eat. It really would not be a major problem.

In this situation, it sounds like Harry is a pretty typical picky five-year-old. While he does not want to eat new things, it is typically not a major ordeal to go out to eat with him. This behavior does not sound outside of the norm.

Dr. Gallo:	Is Harry a picky eater?
Mother:	Yes, and it is pretty difficult to feed him.
Dr. Gallo:	How so?
Mother:	He only eats those square hamburgers from Wendy's and plain rice, nothing else.
Dr. Gallo:	So if you make something else for dinner, such as fish, chicken, or pasta, what does Harry do?
Mother:	He simply refuses to eat it. There were a few times my husband and I told him that he had to eat what we made because I was not going to make him a hot dog. He ended up not having dinner for three nights in a row because he kept refusing.
Dr. Gallo:	What if the family went out for dinner? How would that go?
Mother:	That is a nightmare! We tried going out as a family a few times in the past, but Harry said that the hot dog he got at whatever restaurant we went to was not the same as the one at home, and so he refused to eat it. He then ruined our dinner because he ended up crying, having a temper tantrum, and refusing to eat.

The Harry in the second example is showing significantly more signs and symptoms in regard to eating that would be consistent with an ASD. It is also important to note that in the second example, Harry's eating preferences are truly impacting the family in a very negative way, whereas it is not like that in the first example.

Sensory Integration Issues

If one were to look up sensory integration dysfunction or sensory integration disorder in the *DSM-IV-TR*, one is not going to find anything. In fact, it is not considered a psychological problem at all but more of a subspecialty of occupational therapy. Sensory integration dysfunction is a problem with the five basic senses, touch, taste, smell, sight, and hearing, in addition to the sense of movement, which is handled by the vestibular or balance system in the inner ear, and the positional sense of where the body is in time and space, also known as proprioception.

It is not uncommon for individuals on the spectrum to have sensory integration issues. For example, some of the more common sensory integration issues include the sense of touch, such as being bothered by the tags in clothes, not wanting to wear certain types of clothes or specific materials because they are too itchy or scratchy, or having problems with the seams of the socks. It is important to keep in mind that sensory issues do not have to be a problem area reserved only for individuals on the spectrum. The fact that an individual either has a full-blown sensory integration disorder or may just be showing some specific areas of difficulty does not mean that they have autism.

When my daughter, who does not have autism, was three or four years old and was starting the process of dressing herself in the morning, we had a few instances in which the seams of her socks bothered her to such an extent that she either would have to change her socks a few times in the morning or would have a fit and cry because they did not feel right.

Some children on the spectrum may be so affected by these sensory issues that they only wear a limited array of clothing, which they will wear over and over again, regardless of the cleanliness of the garment or its appropriateness to the weather. They may also hate the feeling of walking on grass, sand, or other specific textures. The textures of foods could also be included in this category. It sometimes happens that a child is a picky eater because they do not like the textures of specific foods, which they find to be disturbing.

Sometimes individuals with sensory integration issues can be quite affected by bright lights, or even lights which others would not consider bright are too bright for them. Some individuals are negatively affected by fluorescent lights and find the rapid flicker extremely disturbing, while the majority of us are simply unaware of it.

These children may also be quite affected by loud noises, such as fireworks, the blender, trash trucks, or the vacuum cleaner. Individuals with sensory integration issues may actually feel these experiences more intensely than the rest of us do and are therefore more significantly affected by them. One must be careful about asking these sensory questions so as to not overpathologize or "read into" issues.

Dr. Gallo:	Does Ron have any problems with loud noises, bright lights, or the texture of clothes?
Mother:	Yes, he always covers his ears when a loud motorcycle goes by.
Dr. Gallo:	Some of those motorcycles can be really loud. Is that a noise that bothers you as well, or do you think maybe Ron's reaction to the noise is more than what would be expected?
Mother:	Oh no, those things are super loud, and I put my hands over my ears as well.
Dr. Gallo:	So Ron's reaction is pretty similar to if not the same as your reaction to loud noises in general and motorcycles in particular.
Mother:	Yes, it is pretty much the same.
Dr. Gallo:	Does Ron have any difficulty with anything else, such as bright lights or clothes?
Mother:	Well, he is picky about his clothes, as he really likes his Darth Vader shirt and wants to wear that all the time.
Dr. Gallo:	Why does he like it so much?
Mother:	Because he really likes *Star Wars*.
Dr. Gallo:	Ok, so he wants to wear the shirt because he likes *Star Wars* so much, not because he likes the texture or feel of the shirt?
Mother:	No, he doesn't have any problems with the texture of things or with tags in his shirts.

In this example, Ron's preferences in shirts and reaction to a loud motorcycle would not be considered outside the norm.

In terms of vestibular and proprioceptive difficulties, does the individual know where their body is in time and space? This type of difficulty can be manifested in a few different ways. For example, is the child clumsy? Do they tend to trip and fall often? Obviously, if one doesn't have a good feel for one's body and has difficulty accurately judging where their feet are in relation to the curb or the next step up the stairs, they are going to have some problems staying on their feet. When the child was younger, would they often step on their parents' toes or bump into them without really intending to do so?

As mentioned in a previous chapter, these children can become "space invaders," by not having any awareness of socially appropriate boundaries, and get much too close for comfort to others.

Pain Tolerance

Keeping with the theme of sensory issues, the specialist should inquire about the patient's pain tolerance. Do they tend to have a pretty typical reaction to pain, or are they either under- or oversensitive? This could be assessed by questions such as "When Ralph was younger and he would fall and get hurt or scrape his knee, what kind of reaction would he have?" While everyone has their own unique reaction to pain, one would typically expect a young child who falls down and scrapes his knee to cry and come find a parent. I saw a young child years ago who fell and fractured his arm but had basically no reaction to it, aside from holding it. It was not until the next day, when significant bruising had developed, that the parents noticed and took him to the doctor.

While that was a rather extreme example, other individuals on the spectrum can have quite different reactions, such as not having any reaction to getting hurt when it is clear that they are hurt, but then having an extreme overreaction to something very minor, such as somebody touching them.

Imitating Others

By the age of two, most typically developing children have an interest in observing and imitating what they see others doing. This can often take the form of a toddler wanting to dust if mom is dusting or help dad when he is raking leaves. When the person being evaluated was that age, did they engage in such activities? Given the fact that we know that children on the spectrum are often referred to as "being in their own world," this could be an interesting differential diagnostic factor. A child who is in their own world would not have any interest in noticing what others are doing, much less imitating that action.

Lining Up Toys

I am unsure as to how this behavior, combined with spinning items such as plates, became one of the main symptoms people identify with autism. However, when looking into this atypical way of playing with toys, it is important that an appropriate level of understanding is achieved. For example, if you meet parents who tell you that their son takes the lids of their Tupperware containers out of the cabinet and lines them up, then that would be a very specific instance of what we are talking about. However, if that same child is lining up his toys, such as blocks, cars, or dinosaurs, additional information is needed.

Dr. Gallo: When Johnny was in preschool or kindergarten, did he line up his toys or arrange them by color or shape?

Parent: Yes, he used to love to take his toy cars and line them up in a row.

Dr. Gallo: When he was lining them up, was he doing that as part of some type of story, such as lining up the cars to get them ready for the Indy 500, or something like that?

Parent: No, not that I could tell.

Dr. Gallo: Would he simply line up the toys as a way of playing with them? Such as lining them up and then walking away? Or would he line them up in order to know where all of his cars are, so that then he could play with them in a creative manner?

Parent: No, he would just line them up and leave.

In this situation, it sounds like the child was engaging in "lining-up" behavior that did not serve any purpose and could be indicative of some spectrum concerns. However, if further questioning led to the information that told you Johnny would line up his toys in order to start playing, then that could be more typical and potentially not indicative of an autistic characteristic.

There are also instances in which children will organize things by color or shape. I often tell the parents I meet that when I make models with my children, I organize the pieces either by color or by shape, in a muffin tin, simply to make it easier for me to know where everything is. That information does not suggest that I am "on the spectrum," just that I like to be organized before starting a new project.

Organizing and "obsessive-compulsive" symptoms, as some parents refer to them, will often manifest themselves during the evaluation if they are part of the child's typical repertoire of behaviors. That is one of the main reasons why I like to have blocks and Legos available in my office during the evaluation. If you have a child in your office who plays with the blocks by lining them up or putting all the triangles in one pile and all the rectangles in another or even separating all the blocks by color, then it does not mean that they have autism but that information needs to be recorded and considered as additional grist for the evaluation mill.

Visual Stims

In the earlier section about sensory integration issues, I mentioned the five main senses for which individuals can have unusual responses. Here I am talking about the children stimulating themselves, either revving themselves up and becoming hyperstimulated or calming themselves down and becoming hypostimulated. An example of the questions that you would want to ask the parents here would be as follows: does Sam ever look at things out of the corners of his eyes, inspect objects very closely, or move his head to look at an object from a different angle? This can be noticed in an evaluation when the individual, often a child, walks around the room looking at objects or people out of the corners of their eyes or moving objects around in front of their face.

Parents may often respond yes here, in that their child is very interested in a new toy and will gaze lovingly at it. That "new toy" stare needs to be differentiated from staring at the wheels of his toy car or at the nib of a pen.

Chapter 12

Differential Diagnosis through
the Lifespan

Given the very complicated nature of the autism spectrum, there are a significant number of confounding and confusing variables that need to be ruled out in order to determine if the person being evaluated is on the autistic spectrum. Before the daunting task of determining if the child has any other type of mental health disorder, aside from an ASD or in addition to it, we need to ensure that the proper spectrum diagnosis is made. Namely, do they have autism, Asperger's disorder, or PDD-NOS?

High-Functioning Autism

In the *DSM-IV-TR*,[1] there is no such diagnostic category as high-functioning autism. According to the *DSM-IV-TR*, one either has autism or not. Needless to say, given the vast breadth of the spectrum, one is, of course, going to come across individuals who are higher functioning or are "less affected" by autism than others. The definition I have heard most often from my fellow professionals in the autism community, in regard to determining if an individual is "high functioning," is that if the patient's cognitive ability is in the "normal" range (i.e., if the patient is not mentally retarded), they could be considered "high functioning."

People with autism have clinically significant impairments in the three areas we previously discussed, that is, socialization, language, and unusual or stereotyped

[1]Reprinted with permission from *the Diagnostic and Statistical Manual of Mental Disorders, Text Revision, Fourth Edition* (Copyright 2000). American Psychiatric Association.

behaviors. It would be quite unusual for an individual to have the same level of impairment in all three areas. For example, one might meet a child who has significant language impairments, as demonstrated by him still being nonverbal at the age of four. This same child could be somewhat more typically developing in his socialization skills and making attempts to overcome his language delay by smiling at and approaching other children but may still be obsessed with Thomas the Train. It is possible that you could evaluate an adult who has made tremendous improvements in the area of language, with his pragmatic skills, but continues to have difficulty making and keeping friends and remains obsessed with bus schedules.

This type of inconsistent developmental improvement is probably one of the factors that often confuses professionals and gives them the false impression that the person they are evaluating is not on the spectrum. It is overly simplistic to think that a 15-year-old boy who was diagnosed with autism at the age of three, received significant services for years, and has made positive strides forward is no longer autistic. I believe a more accurate understanding of this teen's current level of functioning is that the services he received, as well as the hard work everyone has put in with him (the parents, the professionals, the individual himself), has really paid off and made a tremendous difference. With time and services, this teen is no longer as affected by his autism as he was when he was first diagnosed.

When I was in kindergarten, I fell and fractured my wrist. I had a cast on my arm for about a month or so, and then my wrist healed. Does the fact that I no longer walk around with a cast on my arm mean that I never broke it? No. It means that I had a problem and received the appropriate medical intervention, and now I am doing significantly better. Needless to say, there are still some residual effects of my fracture, such as my wrist hurting from time to time.

This is the same as the situation for individuals on the spectrum who have received therapeutic services. Just the fact that the patient you see does not flap his hands or line things up anymore does not mean they are not autistic.

Asperger's disorder

There is one very simple and definitive way to differentiate autism from Asperger's disorder. When your patient was a child, did they have a "clinically significant" general delay in language (e.g., using single words by the age of two years, using communicative phrases by the age of three years)? If the answer to that question is yes, regardless of any other information that is obtained, the person does not have Asperger's disorder. Period. The end. I mentioned earlier in the book that this simple fact can save you a great deal of time and potential embarrassment. A four-year-old child who is not talking does not have Asperger's disorder.

Autistic Disorder versus Asperger's disorder

The information presented above will be helpful in a number of situations but not all, of course. Oftentimes, individuals who did not have a clinically significant language delay come in for evaluations. But there being no language delay does not mean that we can rule out Autistic Disorder just yet. Let's briefly review the diagnostic criteria for both Autistic Disorder and Asperger's disorder.

In order to have an Autistic Disorder, the individual must have at least six symptoms: at least two from the social category, at least one from the language category, and at least one from the behavioral category, for an overall total of six. For Asperger's disorder, the individual needs to have a total of at least three symptoms: at least two from the social category and at least one from the behavioral category. While this ratio is the same as that required for a diagnosis of autism, with Asperger's disorder, there is no need to have a total of at least six symptoms, just three.

One of the areas that I believe confuses a large number of clinicians and can cause a great deal of uncertainty is the language category. As may be recalled, the diagnostic criteria state that the individual needs to have problems in at least one of the following four areas: (1) delay in or lack of language development; (2) problems initiating or sustaining conversations; (3) stereotyped or repetitive usage of language; (4) a lack of appropriate make-believe or socially imitative play. What this does not say, which needs to be kept in mind, is if the individual spoke on time, they have Asperger's disorder and not autism. That oversimplification of the diagnostic criteria can often lead people astray. It is quite possible that you will assess an individual who meets all of the diagnostic criteria in all the three problem areas but also spoke on time. That last bit of information does not change the fact that they meet the criteria for autism and not Asperger's.

Clinicians often associate difficulty carrying on a conversation, or the "little professor syndrome" of lecturing people, as a sign of Asperger's and not autism. However, that is not the case, as once again, there is no language criterion mentioned in the diagnosis of Asperger's. What if you come across an individual who meets all of the diagnostic criteria for autism in terms of socialization deficits and behavioral problems, in addition to lecturing others like a little professor, but did not speak until the age of four? In that case, autism would be the most appropriate diagnosis.

When I meet young children and their parents for an evaluation, the parents typically view Asperger's as a higher-functioning form of autism, and if their child has to be diagnosed as being on the spectrum, they would much rather have him be diagnosed with Asperger's than autism. Parents often almost view these disorders as if they were talking about finding a tumor somewhere in their bodies and hoping that it would be benign and not malignant. I tell the parents, and the patients for that matter, that differentiating between a child who is on the high-functioning end of autism versus having Asperger's is almost like differentiating Coke from Pepsi. I will often ask them, "If you were to go to a restaurant for lunch and order a Coke and the waiter told you they didn't have Coke, only Pepsi, would you walk out?" I don't think I have gotten a yes to that question yet. My point here is that I do not view these two disorders as significantly different, as they generally require the same types of interventions, just as I don't view Coke and Pepsi to be very different.

It is also possible that I may be in the minority of autism professionals who do not view differentiating between high-functioning autism and Asperger's as being as important as making sure the person being evaluated receives the services they so greatly require. There are also certain institutions and school districts that like to split hairs between these two diagnoses, and to them, there is a world of difference between high functioning autism and Asperger's disorder. To some organizations and institutions, it comes down to which labels they provide services for and which they do not.

I have met some children and diagnosed them with Asperger's, only to be told months later that the school district denied them services. When I ask the parents why, they tell me they were told there is no "Asperger's" box on an IEP, only an autism box, and since I did not diagnose them with autism, they do not require autism services. I have had similar experiences with various Regional Centers.

However, keeping this information in mind, there are a few behaviors and characteristics that would suggest the individual is more on the Asperger's side of the spectrum than the autism side, some of which may be the following:

(1) Individuals with average to above-average IQs.
(2) Individuals who want to have friends but simply do not know how to go about doing so. These could be the people who tell you how nice it would be to have friends, but they don't understand the concept of what being a friend is or what it takes to make a friend.
(3) Individuals who talk *at* you about a topic of their interest, instead of talking *with* you. These people could be the stereotyped little professor, such as a first grader who will walk up to other kids on the playground and talk at them in tremendous detail about Pokemon or Thomas the Train.
(4) Individuals with intense areas of interest, which would typically make others consider them smart, such as knowing all of the presidents or knowing a great deal about astronomy.
(5) Adults on the spectrum who are better able to care for themselves and hold down a job. I gave examples in the previous chapter about autistic adults who were only able to hold down entry-level jobs that required very

little if any interaction with the public. A higher-functioning adult with Asperger's would theoretically be better able to adapt to the requirements of their jobs, as long as there are not a large number of social requirements placed upon them.

Autism versus Pervasive Developmental Disorder, Not Otherwise Specified (PDD-NOS)

PDD-NOS is the term used when the individual is displaying enough signs and symptoms of having an ASD to merit some concern from a family member or a professional but does not meet the criteria for either an Autistic Disorder (by having at least six symptoms in the three main areas of socialization, language, and behavior) or three symptoms required for Asperger's disorder (at least two in the social realm and one in the behavioral realm).

This diagnostic label could be used while evaluating a child whose parents report that he did not speak until the age of three (one of the criteria in the language category and also serves to rule out Asperger's disorder) and has a preoccupation with trains. The parents tell you trains are all he wants to talk about, all he wants to play with, and all he wants to watch on television, and he will watch these videos over and over again (which also serves as the one behavioral criterion we need). When you ask about his social skills, the parents tell you that he asks to play with others, interacts well with peers at the park and on the playground at school, will show and bring them things that interest him, and will do nice things for others. The parents only endorse one of the four social areas of difficulty (i.e., that he makes poor eye contact with others and does not understand nonverbal communication or body language).

In this situation, the child is not reported to have the two social symptoms required for either autism or Asperger's. Keep in mind here that while I reported two social difficulties, namely, poor eye contact and not understanding nonverbal communication and body language, both of these are listed as one area of impairment in the *DSM-IV-TR*. However, there are clearly some "autistic-like" behaviors occurring, which need to be identified. This child would be diagnosed as having a PDD-NOS.

Could the diagnosis of PDD-NOS also be used with an older individual who was diagnosed with autism in the past, received a significant amount of services over the years and has made great progress because of those services? Or would diagnosing that person with high-functioning autism be more appropriate, because of the great progress they have made? We always need to keep the patient's history in mind, and that history never changes. If the individual met all of the criteria in the past for a diagnosis of autism, then that would continue to be the most appropriate diagnosis.

The individuals who view Asperger's disorder as a higher-functioning form of autism might think that an autistic individual who has received services and has shown tremendous improvement would now qualify for a diagnosis of Asperger's. While on the surface that may sound reasonable, it really does not make any diagnostic sense. This individual who did not speak until the age of four, but is now highly verbal, still has a developmental history of a speech delay, regardless of how well they are doing years or decades later. That history of a language delay would continue to rule out a diagnosis of Asperger's disorder and suggests that this is a person with a previous diagnosis of autism who is doing very well and is only "mildly affected." In fact, this is really how people are supposed to progress, given the remitting nature of the autism spectrum.

ASDs and/or ADHD

There can be a great deal of overlap between the symptoms of all three forms of ADHD (the combined type, the hyperactive-impulsive type, and the inattentive type) and the ASDs. According to the *DSM-IV-TR*, "Attention-Deficit/Hyperactivity Disorder is not diagnosed if the symptoms of inattention and hyperactivity occur exclusively during the course of a Pervasive Developmental Disorder or a Psychotic Disorder" (p. 91). But what if the signs of ADHD occur separate from the PDD? Before we approach such complicated matters, let's take a closer look at ADHD and how it differs from the autism spectrum.

Individuals who have ADHD need to show at least six of nine symptoms of inattention, hyperactivity/impulsivity, or both before the age of seven. If the child has significant deficits in these areas, it is quite likely that the problems will become much more apparent by the time they enter kindergarten, typically by the age of five. The *DSM-IV-TR* states that in order for a child to have a diagnosis of autism, they need to have displayed the signs and symptoms of problems before the age of three.

In 2002, Diane Kennedy wrote a wonderful book called *The ADHD–Autism Connection*. In the book, she talked about how ADHD is often the problem that is first identified and diagnosed. This is likely because it is the most common of the two and the one most professionals have the greatest awareness of. This would make perfect sense if one figures that it would be quite difficult to not notice the incredibly hyperactive child in your office who is unable to sit still and stop talking. However, while that child may have ADHD, which could account for some of the problems the parents are concerned about, that may be only one piece of the puzzle. ADHD does not explain all of the problems the child is having, such as flipping his pronouns, not having any interest in friends, or being obsessed with ancient Egypt.

On the cover of Kennedy's book, there is a picture of a small, four-piece jigsaw puzzle that needs to be put together. I think that it is a wonderful visual analogy of what professionals in the autism field often do, that is, attempt to put the diagnostic puzzle together. When I meet families and their children, regardless of the age, the parents often tell me that their son or daughter has previously been diagnosed with ADHD, but that doesn't really answer all of their questions and does not seem to accurately explain why their child does what he or she does. This is one of those instances that shows that the parents can be an incredibly helpful source of the information that needs to be considered and respected throughout all steps of the assessment process.

There are several ways in which autism and ADHD can overlap and serve to muddy the diagnostic waters.

The first diagnostic criterion for autism is "marked impairment in the use of multiple nonverbal behaviors such as eye-to-eye gaze, facial expression, body postures, and gestures to regulate social interaction." It is quite possible that a child with any of the three types of ADHD could have problems in this area. For example, how are you going to be able to maintain appropriate eye contact with others if you are very easily distracted or are incredibly active and cannot sit still for any period of time?

I will often ask the parents if their child looks at them when the parents call their name. This is another factor that kids on the spectrum and those with ADHD share. Kids on the spectrum are often thought of as being in their own world and do not respond when people call their name. If the child has great difficulty with attention, it is also likely that they would not respond when their name is called.

What about the ability to read people, such as reading body language and nonverbal communication? This is another typical problem area for both populations. However, with children on the spectrum, they do not understand body language or facial expressions because they usually do not look at the person and often miss their facial cues, or if they do see the cues, they may either not understand them or simply misinterpret them. For a child with ADHD, they could be either too active or too inattentive to notice. Sometimes the children simply are not interested in the other person's body language or choose to ignore it. All of these factors need to be taken into consideration when making a diagnosis.

In terms of making and keeping friends, some children with ADHD want to have friends but do not have any because their hyperactivity or impulsivity serves to distance them from others. Why would Edgar choose to play with Isaac who is overly active and is often getting in trouble at school? What about if Sarah is overly impulsive and always touches peers, or poke them, or does things without thinking? This is very different from the child on the spectrum who either has no interest in making friends or does have an interest but does not know how to appropriately act upon that interest.

Just days before making some changes to this chapter, I met a young boy in kindergarten and his parents for a second opinion on an Asperger's diagnosis. The parents came in because they felt the pediatrician who saw their son, Jack, did not provide them with any quantifiable data, such as an ADOS, to support the diagnosis. As the evaluation continued and I started to collect background information about Jack, he became more agitated and aggressive with his parents. He was making unhappy faces at his mother and was occasionally trying to hit, kick, slap, and lick her. The parents soon told me that toward the end of preschool, Jack was given a one-on-one aide in order to help him to focus, sit in his seat, and follow directions. I was starting to think that we were no longer talking about Asperger's.

I asked the parents to give me just a one- or two-word answer as to what their main concern about Jack was. I would imagine that since we were meeting to talk about Asperger's, the parents would tell me typical Asperger's concerns, such as poor social skills, no friends, and obsessions with something. Both parents quickly told me that their number one concern with Jack was impulse control. While it is not uncommon for kids on the spectrum to have impulse control issues, we were quickly veering away from the autism spectrum and heading toward typical ADHD concerns.

As I dug a little more, the parents told me that they have had numerous meetings with Jack's preschool teachers and were repeatedly told that he has problems focusing, paying attention, completing his work, staying seated, fidgets too much and interrupts the teachers, to name a few. While Jack also had some signs and symptoms that would support a diagnosis of Asperger's disorder (such as no interest in playing with or interacting with peers at home, at church, or at the park, not showing his parents things that interest him, and having a fascination with light switches, ceiling fans, and lawn mowers), this was not the main issue that was causing problems for the family. I left off with the parents being provided with some ADHD rating forms for the two of them as well as for Jack's teachers to fill out and return to their new child therapist to look further into the likelihood that Jack had ADHD, in addition to Asperger's.

In terms of the communication aspects of autism, there can also be an overlap with ADHD. For example, pragmatics is a common area of deficit for children on the spectrum, as they often have difficulty starting or sustaining a back-and-forth conversation with others. This can also be seen with children who have ADHD, as they will interrupt you to talk about what they want to talk about before they forget what they wanted to say, or will "zone out" and not pay attention well enough to converse with you, or become easily distracted, especially if it is not a topic that is of interest to them.

In the previous chapter on other interesting criteria that should be taken into consideration when making a diagnosis, wandering away from the parents was discussed. This is another overlapping area for both the autism spectrum and ADHD. However, there are some subtle differences. Typically, when a small child on the spectrum wanders away from their parents at the mall, the department store, or the park, they are often not upset about having done so. When the parent or the store security finds them, the child is quite happy and content doing whatever they are doing. However, with children who have ADHD, they seem to realize that they are separated from their parents much quicker and become upset over the separation, hopefully decreasing the likelihood of this happening again in the future.

During a recent conversation, Dr. Jerrold Parrish, a local child and adolescent psychiatrist, noted another interesting overlap, with subtle differences, between ADHD and the autism spectrum, namely, "zoning out" during the evaluation. It is not surprising for children or teens to space out during prolonged evaluations. Once again, children on the spectrum are often reported to be "in their own worlds," and children and teens with ADHD, especially the inattentive and combined types, have difficulty paying attention, which is inherent in the disorder. However, oftentimes the individuals with ADHD tend to pay attention to what is said, even though they do not appear to be doing so, while the children on the spectrum are truly doing their own thing. With practice, the professionals begin to notice this difference earlier in the interview.

In fact, one of the factors that helps me to feel more confident about making a diagnosis of an ASD with a patient of any age is when they do not have any questions about what was discussed for the past several hours. A typically developing child or teenager is often at least somewhat actively involved in the assessment process and usually provides you with information and possibly even disagrees with or argues about the validity of your diagnosis. That is typically not the case with individuals on the autism spectrum. I have lost count of the number of times I have met the parents and their children for hours to talk about the child's difficulties and what needs to be done to help them. Some of these suggestions could even be having them switch to a more appropriate classroom or even a more appropriate school. I would imagine that if some doctor told my ten-year-old daughter or six-year-old son that they needed to make such a change, they would have definite thoughts about that, and even if they would not tell the doctor face-to-face in the office how they felt about it, they would at least tell their parents. This is not so with most individuals on the spectrum.

However, I do remember with some fondness a nine-year-old boy whom I diagnosed with autism several years ago who was the exception to this rule. After talking with his parents for several hours about his long history of difficulty making friends, speech delays, and obsessions with various things, I made the diagnosis and explained my reasoning behind the diagnosis to them. The parents agreed with me, but the boy totally disagreed with my diagnosis and did not have any problem telling me his feelings about both my diagnostic skills and myself. Finally, I had to tell him that while I respect his opinion, I have spent the past several years doing these types of evaluations, day in and day out, helping families to understand why their children do the things that they do and that I felt quite sure I was correct. He still was not convinced when he left!

When you meet a family for an evaluation and the individual has previously been diagnosed with ADHD, ask the parents if they think that the ADHD diagnosis fully explains the problems their child is having. More often than not, the answer will be no. This provides you with a good opening to start asking your autism-specific questions.

Another main area that can differentiate an ASD from ADHD is the stereotyped behaviors necessary for a diagnosis of a spectrum disorder. While overlaps can be expected in terms of socialization difficulties and problems with pragmatics for both children on the autism spectrum and those with ADHD, there is no reason for an overlap in this behavioral realm.

A child who has ADHD can have problems making and keeping friends because of their impulsivity, and they may even have a history of an expressive language delay when they were younger, but it would be quite unusual for a child with ADHD to have an "encompassing preoccupation" with something, as an autistic child would. The same could be said for the remaining behaviors in this section: inflexible adherence to specific, nonfunctional routines or rituals; repetitive motor movements; or a persistent preoccupation with parts of objects.

Let me provide some clarifying information here. In the earlier chapter about the behavioral manifestations of autism, specifically in regard to the inflexible adherence to specific, nonfunctional routines or rituals, I gave examples of problems with transitions between tasks or activities, such as stopping watching television and starting eating dinner. While that is not exactly a nonfunctional routine or ritual, this is another area that affects both individuals with ADHD and those on the autism spectrum.

In terms of household routines, oftentimes parents who have children with ADHD, as well as those who have children on the spectrum, have learned that the routine of giving their child a warning of an upcoming change is very helpful in preventing problems and meltdowns. When it is time to leave for school or stop playing on the computer, these parents will say to their children, "OK, we need to leave for school in 10 minutes . . . OK, 5 minutes warning . . . We need to leave in 1 minute. . . OK, time to go." With that being said, while it is common for children and teens with ADHD to have somewhat higher levels of anxiety than "typical" children, the specific "OCD-ish" rituals that children on the spectrum have, such as things needing to be done in a very specific manner, are usually not present.

Other questions that could help to clarify the diagnostic picture include the following: What do the parents say when they come in for the evaluation? Do the areas they are most concerned about revolve around their child having problems at school, such as difficulty paying attention, not staying in their seat, or other ADHD-related symptoms? What about the teachers? If the parents sign a "Release of Information" form and allow you to talk to the teachers, what are the teachers' main concerns? Are the issues they are concerned about mainly occurring in the classroom, such as signs and symptoms that, once again, would be more indicative of ADHD, such as daydreaming, being easily distracted, not completing their homework, not finishing what they start, being very active and fidgety, or having problems staying in their seat? Or do the concerns revolve more around the main social areas consistent with autism, such as not having any friends, not playing with others, being a loner, or having problems interacting with others on the playground?

Now that the mental health community has a greater depth of knowledge to draw upon, I would suggest that it is not terribly uncommon to have a comorbid condition of ADHD and autism. Now that we realize that the fact that a child having autism does not mean that they stand in the corner banging their head against the wall or watching plates spin, we have a better grasp of the difficulties they are facing, same as the problems those in the neurotypcial community face, including ADHD.

I have even come across situations in which a child has first been diagnosed with ADHD, and once that problem is better regulated through the use of medication, the autistic socialization problems become more apparent. Going back to the *ADHD–Autism Connection*, it is quite likely that you will see an individual for an evaluation who has a previous diagnosis of ADHD. In fact, it is almost starting to become common knowledge among professionals in the autism community that if the person you are evaluating has poly-diagnoses (three or more diagnoses, the most common of which include ADHD, OCD, anxiety disorder, depression, expressive language delay, and oppositional defiant disorder), it is quite likely that the professional who previously saw and diagnosed this individual saw only parts of the diagnostic puzzle and not the entire puzzle. It also becomes more likely that the individual is on the autism spectrum and has, as yet, not been identified as such. If you examine a child or a teenager for an autism spectrum disorder and the parents tell you that the child has been given all of the above-mentioned diagnoses but that they still don't fully explain the problem, you should know that you are probably on the right track by looking for an ASD.

ASDs versus Mental Retardation

In the 1990s, it was felt that most children with autism were also mentally retarded. In 2000, the *DSM-IV-TR* stated, "In most cases, there is an associated diagnosis of Mental Retardation, which can range from mild to profound. There may be abnormalities in the development of cognitive skills (p. 71, APA)." No percentile is given as to how many individuals with autism also have mental retardation.

Today, we need to take this information with a grain of salt and keep in mind that the *DSM-IV* was written more than 15 years ago. At that time, the prevalence rate of autism was between 2 and 5 per 10,000, and Asperger's disorder was so rare that we did not even have any data on prevalence rates. In the *DSM-IV-TR*, it was reported that the median rate of Autistic Disorder was 5 per 10,000, with the reported rates ranging from 2 to 20 per 10,000. There were still no prevalence rates for Asperger's as of the publication of the *DSM-IV-TR*.

In the past 15 years, a great deal of new information has been presented, including a dramatic increase in the number of children being diagnosed with an ASD. For example, at the time I am writing this, the CDC estimates that 1 in every 150 children has an ASD. That is a dramatic difference from between 2 and 5 per 10,000.

There has been a great deal of discussion in the professional community as to whether the increase in the rate of autism diagnoses is due to the recent labeling of the people who were previously diagnosed with mental retardation as having autism. Be that as it may, it is important to accurately determine if the person, in addition to having mental retardation, has autism.

There really is not a great deal of diagnostic overlap between autism and mental retardation. Looking closer at the diagnostic criteria for both, autism is a combination of socialization, language, and behavioral problems, while mental retardation consists of having an IQ below 70, with "concurrent deficits or impairments in present adaptive functioning . . . in at least two of the following areas: communication, self-care, home living, social/interpersonal skills, work, leisure, health, and safety."

Let's look at this situation through the various possible scenarios in which this child could be presented for an evaluation: (1) The child has autism, and there is concern that they may also be mentally retarded. (2) The child is mentally retarded, and there are concerns they may have autism. (3) It is unknown if the person has either autism or mental retardation, but both need to be looked at.

Let's start with the first scenario. You are seeing an individual of any age with autism, and there is a question of a dual diagnosis of mental retardation. The first and foremost issue you are going to face is the fact that all of our "gold standard" IQ tests, such as the Stanford–Binet and Wechsler tests, are standardized tests whose norms are based on a "neurotypical population" and not an autistic population. Depending upon how affected the individual is by their autism, the testing may or may not provide an accurate IQ score. If you evaluate a high-functioning autistic individual or someone with Asperger's, it is possible that the spectrum may not get in the way of obtaining a relatively accurate measure of their IQ. The problem you are going to face is this: if the individual is affected by moderate-to-severe autism and they are found to have an IQ score below 70, thereby meeting the cognitive requirement for a diagnosis of mental retardation, is that number accurate? How are you going to be able to determine how much of that low score is due to a true cognitive deficit and how much is due to the autism? Unfortunately, I don't believe we have found an answer to that question yet.

I tend to not give individuals who are quite affected by autism an IQ test because the validity of the scores you obtain is likely to be quite low, and it often becomes extremely difficult, if not impossible, to administer the test in the way in which it is meant to be administered, in order to provide standardized results. In these situations, the individuals who are extremely affected by their autism are often receiving a great deal of services already, including services they would receive if a diagnosis of mental retardation had been made.

Earlier this year, the parents of a five-year-old boy who is affected by moderate-to-severe autism wanted me to give him an IQ test in order to help them in determining appropriate school placement. Keeping in mind that this child does not make any eye contact, has tremendous difficulty sitting still for more than a moment or two, and needs to be reinforced and physically prompted to respond most of the time, I knew this was not going to be easy, but I figured I would give it the old college try.

Typically when intelligence tests are administered, it is just the examiner and the patient, alone. I knew that there was no way that was going to work in this case; so I had both the mother and the behaviorist stay in the room. Within minutes, Sam was out of his seat, flapping his hands and needing to be redirected back to the task at hand. I was only able to administer a few of the nonverbal subtests to Sam, but the incredible deviations from the standardized way in which subtests should be administered made the results invalid in my mind.

If we were simply to take the obtained scores at face value, they would definitely place him within the mentally retarded range in terms of his cognitive ability. However, his autism was so pronounced that it made it impossible for me to administer the IQ test in the way it was supposed to be administered. Therefore, while I know Sam is definitely not functioning at an age-appropriate level, I don't feel comfortable saying that he is mentally retarded because of how severely his autism is affecting him.

In regard to the second scenario, that is, needing to determine if a person who has mental retardation also has autism, there are more "tools" available to the professional to help answer that question. The diagnostic criteria for mental retardation, once again, requires adaptive behavior deficits in at least two areas, which could, but do not have to, include the socialization and communication issues common with autism. However, during your meeting with the person and in the history you obtain from the parents or the caregivers, what is the person's socialization like? A six-year-old boy with mild mental retardation, which is considered to encompass 85% of the people with mental retardation, (*DSM-IV-TR*, p 43) might not be able to keep up with his peers intellectually, but that does not mean that he would not be interested in making friends and socializing with others. He may be more interested in playing with toys that same-aged peers of average intellect would not be interested in, but he would not necessarily be the aloof, disinterested-in-others child, which would be characteristic of someone with autism.

It is possible for a child with mental retardation to have language deficits similar to those of children with autism. However, one of the main differentiating factors between a child with autism and one with mental retardation would be the stereotyped patterns of behavior, interests, and activities found mainly in children on the autism spectrum. If the parents or the caregivers do not report any of these stereotyped behaviors, such as obsessions with certain things, significant problems with changes, repetitive movements, or a fascination with parts or pieces of things, a diagnosis of autism cannot be made.

If we were to go back in the child's life to when they were in preschool, kindergarten, or elementary school, there should be several factors that would differentiate these two disorders. At that young age, a child with autism would have shown signs of the disorder, depending upon the severity of their condition. An autistic child at a Mommy and Me class would probably not do what the other children are doing and would not show much interest in interacting with others. That should typically not be the case for a child with mental retardation.

While an autistic child and a child with mental retardation may have the same type of expressive language delay, if the child is fascinated by spinning objects such as fans, or lines up objects, or does not respond when their name is called, then that would be more suggestive of autism.

While it is quite likely that the mentally retarded child's cognitive delays will become apparent when they enter preschool and kindergarten, some of the social and behavioral signs of autism would be present even earlier, especially if you know where to look and the proper questions to ask.

How would the autism–mental retardation question present itself with a teenager or an adult? Once again, the easiest way to determine if the adult you are seeing has mental retardation would be to give them an IQ test. However, we would need to keep in mind that we are utilizing a standardized test to assess a nonstandardized individual.

I once met a 40-year-old woman for an autism evaluation. I was able to meet her entire, very large, family and review all of her past assessments. For the past 40 years, it was thought that she was mentally retarded. That seemed to explain all the difficulties she was having, such as not being able to live on her own, take care of herself, or hold down a steady job.

While her previous intelligence tests did find her to be functioning around the mildly mentally retarded range, there were numerous signs and symptoms of autism that had only recently begun to be considered as playing a role in the problems she had. These factors included not speaking until she was five years old, never playing appropriately with peers when she was younger (whenever she would play with others, she would end up assaulting them), having a long history of obsessions with various objects, and engaging in repetitive hand movements such as flapping her hands.

When these factors are considered, it starts to muddy her diagnostic picture. It suggests that her previous diagnosis of mental retardation with some obsessive-compulsive traits does not answer all of our questions. My determination that she has autism serves to bring into question the validity of her previous IQ tests. Now another complicating question could be how much of the difficulty that she faces while caring for herself is due to her cognitive impairments and how much is due to her autism.

Fragile X, Down's Syndrome, and Other Chromosomal and Genetic Problems

This section is quite complex and outside the realm of expertise for many professionals, including myself. Those who are not geneticists or physicians with extensive knowledge of genetics will need to refer their patients to specialists in those areas. Given that fact, I am always quite wary of making a diagnosis of an ASD if the individual has been previously diagnosed with some type of genetic or chromosomal problem.

Working in a large medical setting such as Kaiser-Permanente, I am lucky enough to be able to refer these individuals to a geneticist for a final determination to answer the question: is there any genetic or chromosomal issue that is causing or exacerbating the patient's autistic-like symptoms?

Fragile X syndrome is a deficit on the X chromosome. According to the Web site of the National Fragile X Foundation (www.FragileX.org), Fragile X syndrome can cause a child to have autism or an ASD, though not all children with Fragile X syndrome have autism or an ASD. The Web site goes on to report the following facts: "For between 2% and 6% of all children diagnosed with autism, the cause is the Fragile X gene mutation. Approximately one-third of all children diagnosed with Fragile X syndrome also have some degree of autism. Fragile X syndrome is the most common known single gene cause of autism." This information tells us that a comorbid condition of autism and Fragile X is possible and should be looked into further. This does not mean that if a patient has Fragile X, they cannot have autism, as was previously thought.

Down's syndrome, also called trisomy 21, is caused by the presence of an extra chromosome on the 21st chromosome. The latest statistics suggest that Down's syndrome occurs in 1 of every 800–1000 births. There are many physical characteristics that are common in individuals with Down's syndrome, such as almond-shaped eyes, poor muscle tone, and a protruding tongue. It is also not uncommon for individuals with Down's syndrome to have mild to moderate mental retardation.

One important factor that is not noted as prevalent in individuals with Down's syndrome is any of the social difficulties consistent with autism. As silly as it may seem, when most people think about Down's syndrome, they probably think about Chris Burke, the actor with Down's who played Corky on the late 1980s' television show *Life Goes On*. While individuals with Down's syndrome, or any other medical or genetic problem for that matter, may be faced with some social difficulties in regard to interacting with people who are not affected by their illness, those individuals would typically be expected to have an interest in interacting with, being friends with, and socializing with peers who also have Down's or similar issues. In fact, children with Down's syndrome tend to be very social. This is not the case for children with autism.

In all of the autism evaluations I have conducted, I have only seen a handful of children with Down's syndrome. I remember when I met with my first child with Down's, a preteen boy, for an evaluation. I told his parents that while I knew a great deal about autism, seeing a child with Down's syndrome for an evaluation was new to me. I then let them know that I felt much better having a Down's syndrome expert in the room helping me to conduct the evaluation. When the parents gave me a funny look, most probably wondering if I was having some sort of visual hallucination (seeing someone in the room who was not there), I told them the expert I was referring to was them.

If you think about it, these parents have interacted with a significant number of children and teens with Down's syndrome and have a much better sense of what is "normal" in terms of Down's syndrome than the majority of us do. One of the most telling and pertinent questions I asked this boy's mother was about the times when he was in the special Mommy and Me class for children with Down's. I asked her what her son was like and how he interacted with his peers with Down's. It became quite clear to the mother that while her son is different from his same-aged peers without Down's, he is also quite different from his peers with Down's syndrome. She recalled that while the other children in her son's class had various levels of developmental delays, they were all quite social and happy, but her son was not. While all the mothers and children were engaging in group activities during circle time, her son was off doing his own thing and did not want to be part of the group. This child was also in special education classes for children with Down's syndrome and other medical problems throughout elementary school. During those years in early elementary school, this boy did not interact with his peers, did not have friends, and would often be off, doing his own thing.

The other child with Down's syndrome I saw for an evaluation was a young girl who also has mental retardation. Once again, I was able to utilize the parent's knowledge and past experiences about Down's in order to help all of us obtain a better understanding of the problems she was facing. The diagnosis of autism was made after the mother was able to provide me with detailed information about her daughter's social deficits, as well as language delays and intense interests in letter boards and the color yellow.

Information about autism and Down's syndrome is quite difficult to obtain, mostly probably for a variety of reasons, including the rarity of the two disorders being comorbid. In a 2001 article written by George T Capone, M.D., of the Down Syndrome Clinic in Maryland, for the Down's Syndrome Association newsletter, it was estimated that between 5% and 7% of individuals with Down's also have an ASD. This number is substantially higher than that for the general population, which is less than 1%. This number marks a significant step forward in the acknowledgement that these two disorders can coexist, something that was not considered in the past and is not considered even today among many professionals.

Schizoid Personality Disorder versus Autism

What do you call a person who does not have any friends, does not have any interest in making friends, and has no desire to interact with others? Well, if that individual were a child or a teen and they also had some type of repetitive behaviors or encompassing preoccupation with something, you would diagnose them with either autism (if there were also language issues) or Asperger's disorder (if there were no language issues). However, what if we are talking about an adult? While this sounds like the case of a previously undiagnosed adult with autism, it also fits into the category of Schizoid Personality Disorder.

According to the *DSM-IV-TR*, a Schizoid Personality Disorder is defined as "[a] pervasive pattern of detachment from social relationships and a restricted range of expression of emotions in interpersonal settings, beginning by early adulthood (p. 694)." The definition goes on to state that the disorder does not occur during the course of a PDD.

In the "differential diagnosis" section for Schizoid Personality Disorder, it states, "There may be great difficulty differentiating individuals with Schizoid Personality Disorder from those with milder forms of Autistic Disorder and from those with Asperger's disorder. Milder forms of Autistic Disorder and Asperger's disorder are differentiated by more severely impaired social interactions and stereotyped behaviors and interests (p. 696)."

While I would imagine that there may be a number of adults who would meet those criteria, what about those adults who are autistic but have never been identified or diagnosed as such? We need to consider the history of autism and the simple fact that as early as 1994 when the *DSM-IV* was published the diagnosis of autism was, at the most, 1 per 2000 people and that there was very little, if any, awareness that the spectrum was as broad as we now know it to be.

I believe it is possible, if not likely, that the majority of adults who have been previously diagnosed as having a Schizoid Personality Disorder are really individuals with autism who went undiagnosed as children and teenagers and have since been misdiagnosed. I further believe there are ways to prove or disprove this hypothesis. First, the diagnostic criteria for a Schizoid Personality Disorder states that this pervasive pattern of detachment . . . must have begun by early adulthood. If the individual has autism, their social difficulties must, by definition, have begun by early childhood.

If you meet an adult who has previously been diagnosed as having a Schizoid Personality Disorder and whom you think may, in actuality, have autism, you are going to need additional history. You will want to hear from the patient and the people who knew him well when he was a child, such as his parents, older siblings, or other relatives. Given the nature of the diagnosis, it is somewhat unlikely that this person (most likely a man) would have a girlfriend or wife for you to talk to. If there is such a significant other, the mere fact that this person exists in the patient's life is diagnostically relevant and should be taken into consideration.

Does this individual have additional history that would support an autism diagnosis? Were there social difficulties present when they were very young or did they develop in adolescence or early adulthood? What about early development, such as verbal milestones? A grown man diagnosed with a Schizoid Personality Disorder who has had those symptoms all of his life and did not talk until he was four years old is beginning to sound significantly more like a person with autism that has been misdiagnosed.

There is nothing in the diagnostic criteria for Schizoid Personality Disorder that mentions either language or behavioral idiosyncrasies. Does the patient have a history of encompassing preoccupations with things, problems with changes in routines, or hand flapping when they were younger? What about the other interesting autistic-like characteristics previously mentioned, such as being a very picky eater, having sensory integration issues, or having problems holding down a job? The more factors this person has, the more likely it is that a diagnosis of autism would be more accurate. It is quite possible that if you are seeing an adult for an evaluation to determine the reason for his social difficulties, they could have been previously diagnosed with a Schizoid Personality Disorder, as that would be the most logical assumption to make without enough knowledge about how the autism spectrum manifests itself in adults.

Social Phobia versus ASD

"He's just shy" is something I hear from parents quite often. Parents will bring their child in for an evaluation because the teacher or the pediatrician has concerns about their lack of socializing with peers. A large number of people of all ages are shy, and that does not place them on the autism spectrum. However, at what point does being incredibly shy become part of the spectrum?

The differential diagnosis between an ASD (or Schizoid Personality Disorder) and social phobia states that for individuals with either of these two diagnoses, social situations are avoided because of a lack of interest in interacting with or relating to others. This is very different from individuals with social phobias who "have a capacity for and interest in social relationships with familiar people" (*DSM-IV-TR*, p. 455). The *DSM-IV-TR* goes even further to state, "for children to qualify for a diagnosis of Social Phobia, they must have at least one age-appropriate social relationship with someone outside the immediate family."

With the autism spectrum, socialization difficulties are only one of three major components necessary for a diagnosis. The shyness and social avoidance of a socially phobic child or teen may account for them not looking at people when they speak to them or being afraid to approach strangers or even talk to you during the evaluation. However, we would need to look further into their history for additional information before making a diagnosis of an ASD. Some of the questions we would need the answers to would include the following: Have they always been that way? When they were a young child at the age of two or three and their parents would take them to the park to play, would they approach and play with other children, or would they simply hide behind their parents and not interact with peers? When they were in preschool, kindergarten, and elementary school, were they shy and reserved at first, which is quite typical, and then "warmed up" to others as time progressed? Or did they remain aloof and continue to rebuff the advances of same-aged peers, or even those of teachers and yard aides, for that matter?

While the shared deficits in socialization for both an ASD and social phobia are somewhat apparent, there could also be shared communication deficits in the area of pragmatics. Is it possible that this socially phobic child or teen cannot carry on a conversation with you because they are too shy? Possibly. If they were socially anxious, this unwillingness or inability to converse would typically apply to people outside the home or to people they did not know very well. If the deficit with pragmatics persists even for people the individual does know well, then that could be more indicative of autism. Obviously, if this shy individual who has difficulty talking with new people also has a history of delayed language development, in addition to flipping their pronouns or echolalia, we are moving much more rapidly into the realm of autism.

One of the main factors that differentiates children with an ASD from those with social phobia is the repetitive or stereotyped behaviors that are not characteristic of social phobia.

Imagine you see a teenager whose parents report that he has a long history of social anxiety. As you dig deeper in your interview with the teen and the parents, you find out that he has a long history of avoiding others and has never truly had any interest in making friends. In fact, he remains very happy to sit in his room reading science books and watching all six *Star Wars* movies over and over again. The father tells you that before he became interested in *Star Wars*, he was obsessed with dinosaurs, and everyone thought he knew so much about dinosaurs that he was going to become a paleontologist when he grew up. "By the way," his mother says, "he was also very late in his developmental milestones, especially his speech, as he didn't talk until he was 4 years old." Now the teen you are meeting to look at social phobia also happens to have several of the diagnostic criteria that place him more in the autistic realm than the anxious realm.

Depression versus ASD

It would not surprise any mental health professional that a person who is depressed may manifest that depression in several different ways, including becoming more reserved and not wanting to socialize with others. If that depression and social alienation occur over a long period of time, it may become a concern that could be brought up in an evaluation. One rather simple way to differentiate social alienation or aloofness because of depression from that due to a spectrum disorder would be to ask the person and/or those who accompanied them to the evaluation to think back to before this depression began.

If you are evaluating a teen or an adult, you would always want to take them back in time to when they were in preschool, kindergarten, or elementary school. How was their socializing at that time? Imagine you are meeting a depressed and moody 15-year-old. You might want to proceed something like this.

Dr. Gallo: Mom, you were telling me that Stephanie doesn't really have any interest in seeing her friends or socializing with others on the weekend. Is that right?

Mother: Yes.

Dr. Gallo: How long has that been going on for?

Mother: Maybe a few years.
Dr. Gallo: OK, so then let's not focus on these past few asocial years for awhile and let's back up to when Stephanie was in kindergarten or early elementary school. What was she like then?
Mother: Oh, she was totally different. She had so many friends, and she was very popular. I remember she would have play dates often and would always be asking me if a friend could come over or if she could go over to another girl's house. That is why I am so concerned about her now. She just seems so different.

Given the information that the mother provided, Stephanie does not have the long-standing socialization deficits necessary for a diagnosis of an ASD. However, had the mother reported that her daughter's social aloofness started in kindergarten or elementary school and persisted to this day, additional information would need to be obtained to truly rule out a spectrum disorder.

To complicate matters further, what if you were faced with a depressed child and it would not be feasible to look back in time to when they were in kindergarten and elementary school, since that is their current age? We could always revert to "plan B," namely, the behavioral issues that would be consistent with autism but not depression. There should be no reason why a depressed child should also have a history of obsessions with things (except for potentially morbid thoughts that could also be signs of depression), significant problems dealing with changes to routines, repetitive movements, or intense interests in parts or pieces of things. If these behavioral difficulties are not present, a diagnosis of autism or Asperger's would not be warranted.

Expressive Language Delay versus ASD

A speech delay is a primary reason why most children are referred to me for an autism evaluation. However, as the famous saying goes, "sometimes a cigar is just a cigar," and sometimes a speech delay is just a speech delay.

When I meet the parents of these children for the evaluation, I let them know that whoever made the referral (the pediatrician, the teacher, or the therapist) simply wants to make sure that there is nothing else going on with their child, aside from their delayed speech. That serves the dual purpose of putting them more at ease and helping them to appreciate the fact that other people care about their child and want to make sure they are doing the best they can. While delayed speech does fulfill the communication criteria for a diagnosis of an ASD, significantly more information is needed before such a diagnosis can be made.

You are going to want to ask if the child has the significant social deficits necessary for such a diagnosis. It is quite possible for the child's inability to communicate effectively with peers to alienate them from others, but that does not need to be the case. If we are talking about a three year old who only has minimal language and does not interact with peers at school, do they interact with others at the park or when friends come over for play dates? For that matter, does the child have any friends?

A typical child with an expressive language delay would also be more likely to rely on gestures, such as pointing, in order to get his or her needs met, something not always seen with children on the spectrum. Does the child you are evaluating point out things that interest them to others? Do they call attention to a pretty cloud or a squirrel at the park? Children on the spectrum, depending upon how affected they are, are less likely to show and bring things that interest them to others (one of the aforementioned socialization criteria). It also does not take any language whatsoever for a young child to pick a flower and give it to their parents or draw something and give it to them. Once again, these behaviors are more common among neurotypical children.

If you were to take the "typical" American family (whomever that might be) with a young child and move them to Germany or Japan where they do not speak the language, the child would most probably find a way to communicate with his peers. An English-speaking child playing in a park in Paris could smile at and approach others, as well as share toys. In that situation, the language difference is not much of a barrier. If the parents tell you that their language-delayed child does not have any friends, and further interviewing reveals that the child was quite social in the past but no longer attempts to interact with peers due to numerous rejections because of his speech, then that would sound more like the child has stopped attempting to socialize because of discouragement, not autism.

Another main area that differentiates the child with autism from a child who only has an expressive language delay is the presence of any of the repetitive or stereotyped behaviors. A child with a language delay, who also has significant problems with changes to routines and a history of flapping his hands, would raise some red flags that would need to be looked at in greater detail.

Oppositional Defiant Disorder (ODD) versus ASD

Some children and teens with ODD share several characteristics in common with their counterparts on the spectrum, mainly in the social areas. The parents might tell you their child does not look at them in the eye when they talk to them or does not seem able to read others' emotions or body language.

As the interview continues, you might be informed that the child or the teenager does not make good eye contact with their parents. However, as you dig deeper, you are told that this behavior mainly occurs only when the individual is being disciplined by the parent. This finding is very common among people of all ages and is not indicative of an ASD. It is typical human behavior to not want to look at someone directly in the eyes when they are upset with you. Just think about where you were looking when you were a child and your teacher or parents were upset with you.

The parents may tell you their child does not understand nonverbal communication or body language. However, the reason they came to this conclusion is that the child does not try to comfort their mother when she is sad about their behavior or does not acknowledge when someone is upset. It may be made clearer with additional questioning, such as by looking back in their history, that while the ability to do so is there, the child is simply choosing not to care about or not to be interested in others' feelings at times.

There is no reason why a child or teenager with ODD would not be interested in making or playing with friends. While it is quite possible that their oppositional approach to interacting with others will quickly sour their relationship with playmates or peers, the desire to interact would still be there. This finding should carry significant weight in terms of a differential diagnosis. There should also be no reason why the ODD child would not want to show or bring things that interest them to others, such as parents, unlike the child on the spectrum, who would potentially be "in their own world."

The oppositional child may have extreme temper tantrums, similar to a child on the spectrum, especially in regard to changes. This is another area in which specific questioning is needed. When I ask parents how their child deals with changes to routines or transitions, they often say, "Terribly, especially when I need him to stop doing what he is doing, such as watching television and do something else, like homework." This finding is not surprising and encompasses a large number of people of all ages. Who wants to stop doing an enjoyable activity and start doing something they do not want to do? You will need to inquire about other instances of change that would not be so upsetting to a typical child. One example could be changing around their going-to-bed routine, such as asking them to go to the bathroom before brushing their teeth, instead of the other way around. Another example would be asking if the child would become upset if something was moved in the living room or if Mom and Dad switched seats at the dinner table. While these changes could be issues for children on the spectrum, they would typically not be a problem for more neurotypical children.

What about the more innocuous changes, such as changing something around the house, moving a picture, or some minor redecorating? We would need to combine all of this information to form a clearer picture of the child.

I recently saw a wonderful little five-year-old girl for therapy, who was a holy terror at home. The parents were at a loss as to how to control her terrible acting-out behavior. The interesting part of the story was that she was wonderful at school and a model student. This fact gave me the information I needed to hypothesize that maybe there is something that needs to be changed at home in order to better help the parents to deal with their daughter, as the school seems to know what needs to be done. If a child has autism, they have it in all environments, including home, school, daycare, and church. It is also possible that this girl was using up all of her internal resources to "keep it together" at school and would simply "lose it" at home. However, if she were to be sufficiently on the spectrum to warrant a diagnosis, the school should have also noticed problematic behaviors.

Selective Mutism versus ASD

A child with selective mutism could possibly appear to have autism to a teacher or a frustrated parent who does not understand why their child is not talking at school or in other social situations. This could be a child who hides behind their parents and does not answer any of the questions their teacher or doctor asks of them.

There are a few factors that could help differentiate a child with selective mutism from a child with an ASD. If the child does not want to talk to adults or groups of children, how about in a one-on-one setting? Does the child have any friends? When they are at home, do they talk about their friends or peers who they wish were their friends? The selectively mute child would typically be totally fine talking with family members at home. Hence the term "selective." However, it is more likely that the child on the spectrum would remain more consistent in their unwillingness or hesitancy to talk or interact, regardless of the setting.

Along similar lines, does this child wish they were better able to talk to others, or are they quite happy and content to keep to themselves? A child more moderately affected by autism may not have any interest in speaking to others and would be totally content not interacting. Children toward the higher end of the spectrum, including some children with Asperger's syndrome, may want to have friends but do not know how to go about doing so.

Given the nature of the condition and the fact that the child is most likely not going to talk to you, you would need to find out from the parents if the child is happy with the way things are, or would they like to change their situation and become more social? What about people whom the child is more familiar with? Do they ask to see same-aged peers such as cousins or children of friends of the family whom they know well? If so, that would argue against a diagnosis of an ASD and would be more suggestive of selective mutism.

Was there any type of precipitating event that may have caused the child to become anxious or mute, or have they always been that way? If your questioning uncovers the fact that the child has been selectively mute at school for the past year since their father was incarcerated or since their mother died of cancer, you now have somewhat of a logical reason for this behavior, which mitigates against autism.

How was the child's language development? Are they displaying any of the unusual verbal signs of a spectrum disorder, aside from being unable or unwilling to converse with others? Any history of echolalia, flipping pronouns, or lecturing others? Could the child possibly have some type of more typical speech difficulty, which makes them embarrassed to talk in front of others, such as a lisp, stutter, or stammer?

As noted with previous differential diagnoses, there should be no specific reason for a child with selective mutism to display any of the behavioral peculiarity that children with autism display. Did they play with toys appropriately and in a creative manner when they were younger? Do they have difficulty with transitions, encompassing preoccupations with certain objects or topics, repetitive movements, or preoccupations with parts of objects? If some or any of these behaviors are present, then we might be steering away from selective mutism.

OCD versus ASD

One of the most common psychiatric diagnoses I have noticed which children on the spectrum receive, before being diagnosed with autism, is OCD. It may be easier for a parent or a professional to overlook some delayed milestones or minimal socializing with peers, especially if this is the parents' first child. However, when the child becomes "obsessed" with Thomas the Train and wants to watch it all day, every day or spends prolonged periods of time lining up cars or objects or playing with water for hours, then that behavior becomes much more noticeable and much harder to ignore.

While individuals with OCD and ASDs may look very similar in that they can engage in their obsessive thoughts or compulsive behaviors for prolonged periods of time, the underlying issue driving them is very different. If your patient with OCD is a teen or an adult, at some point they realize this behavior is causing them problems and want to stop doing it. However, an individual on the autism spectrum does not have any difficulty with their behavior and most probably has absolutely no interest in changing or stopping it.

If a child has obsessive thoughts about a certain topic, such as death or being afraid of throwing up, or they have a compulsion to line things up or not step on cracks in the sidewalk, then that may not necessarily preclude them from being able to socialize with or do nice things for others. However, if their obsessive lining up of objects or their obsessive interest in Pokemon also includes an inability for them to talk about anything else and has been present since the age of 3, additional information would need to be obtained to further rule out an ASD.

During the course of a hypothetical evaluation with an adult, you are told by a parent that their child is obsessed with *The Lord of the Rings*. Ever since he was a little boy, there were topics and objects that would consume an inordinate amount of his time, much more so than other topics would interest his siblings. This person may be "obsessed" with *The Lord of the Rings*, as shown by him knowing a great deal about it, but that would not qualify as an obsession in terms of an OCD, because of the fact that it does not cause him "marked distress . . . or significantly interfere with the person's normal routine" (*DSM-IV-TR*, p. 463).

Could this individual, as a child, talk about other topics or show or bring things to his parents, aside from objects directly related to this topic? Was this all they would talk about? Would he lecture others about this specific area of interest and be oblivious to others' nonverbal cues that they are not interested in what he is talking about? Did he have difficulty making and keeping friends in elementary school because that topic was all he would talk about? Did he have other friends whom he would interact with during recess and lunchtime at school and not talk about this "obsessive" topic?

By obtaining the answers to these questions, you should be able to determine the answers to three major questions: Were these "obsessions" or "compulsions" activities or thoughts that caused him marked distress, thereby potentially qualifying him for an OCD diagnosis? Were the obsessions or compulsions things that he really enjoyed engaging in and talking about? If so, that would be more consistent with the autism spectrum and rule out OCD. Finally, was this person simply really into his hobby and does not qualify for any type of diagnosis?

If you come across a child with previous diagnoses of OCD (for being obsessed with butterflies), inattentive-type ADHD (for zoning out and being in his own world), and an expressive language delay (because he did not talk until the age of 4), it is likely that the previous professionals were only looking at one specific part of the diagnostic puzzle and did not take the necessary step backward to obtain a more encompassing and comprehensive picture. Even without starting to collect your own history of this child, you know he already meets the language criteria for autism because of talking late, the behavioral criteria because of his obsession with butterflies, and potentially one of the two necessary components for socialization difficulties by being in his own world.

Chapter 13

Feedback for the Patient and the Family/Parents

Now that you have spent the past several hours asking numerous, in-depth questions of your patient and the historians who have come with them, in addition to possibly calling several other people who were not present at the meeting, you hopefully have a comprehensive picture of the problems the individual is facing, as well as the knowledge of their early developmental history. The main question that needs to be answered at this point is "Have all of your questions been answered sufficiently to give you enough data to answer the referral question, that is, 'Does this individual have an ASD?'"

There are times when that question is as difficult to answer as the referral question. Were you able to obtain all the background information you needed to come to a well-thought-out conclusion that is supported by both the historical information you obtained and your clinical observations of the patient in your office?

Did you need to administer any quantifiable assessment measures, such as the ADOS, the ADI-R, an IQ test, or the Vineland-II, which is a measure of adaptive behavior? If you did administer these measures, were the scores you obtained consistent with the information provided by the patient (both verbally and visually), the parents, and any other historian you were able to contact?

Was the client's behavior helpful in making your decision, and was their presentation consistent with the information you obtained? Let's say that for the past two hours, your patient's parents have told you that their child makes wonderful eye contact and does not have a history of flapping their hands. Is that information consistent with their behavior during your time with them, or was the child's behavior different from what the parents reported? Meeting a child who wanders around your office for the entire time flapping their hands and spinning objects would be a dead giveaway as to their diagnosis but is rather unlikely to happen. Maybe your patient made wonderful eye contact, was able to read your body language, and interacted very appropriately with the people in the room. All of this information needs to be taken into consideration and plays an integral part in the formation of your conclusion.

However, while there will surely be times when a definitive answer can be given, there will also be instances in which you simply cannot come to a conclusion, yet. When I was in graduate school, my first clinical supervisor was a brilliant psychologist named Kathy Sullivan. One of the most enduring pieces of advice she gave me so long ago was to listen to my gut and follow my instincts. I mention Dr. Sullivan's words of wisdom because I still follow her advice today. Please don't misinterpret this to suggest that I simply look at the patient in my office and decide upon a diagnosis by what feels right. Even after administering all the instruments and asking all the questions you can think of, you may not yet be 100% convinced of a diagnosis. There are times when, for some reason, you simply do not have enough information to be definitive. Maybe the parents were not good historians, or maybe they did not want to come to the evaluation and only did so because the doctor or the teacher "made them."

If you are not ready to make a final determination, don't. I often tell parents that I would like to obtain additional information before coming to any conclusion about their child. When I first started conducting autism evaluations, I used to think that the parents would be upset or annoyed with me after having spent several hours talking to me and answering all of my in-depth questions just to be told that I don't have any answers for them. I was also concerned that the parents might view my lack of a definitive diagnosis as a sign that I did not know what I was doing. Luckily, the exact opposite tends to happen when I tell parents I would like to obtain more information before coming up with a diagnosis, to make sure I fully understand what is happening with their child so as to provide them with as thorough an evaluation as possible. I then typically ask the parents to sign a few "Release of Information" forms to allow me to talk with others, such as teachers and relatives, who know the child or the teen well. If I am meeting an adult for an evaluation, I would like to be able to speak with coworkers, supervisors, friends, or relatives if they would allow me to do so.

The situations in which it is significantly more difficult to provide a definitive diagnosis tends to happen more in meetings with the family of a very young child. There are times when either the child is simply too young or the symptoms are not prominent enough to warrant a diagnosis and possibly traumatize the parents. In situations in which the child is very young, such as a two-year-old with a language delay (which was the identified problem that got them to see me), I am sometimes unable to form a definitive conclusion about a diagnosis at that time.

In those situations, I will instruct the parents to contact the local Regional Center to have the child evaluated there as well. While I believe it would be rather unlikely that the Regional Center would make a diagnosis if the symptoms were so minor, they would typically provide the child with speech therapy, as it is likely that speech is one of the main problem areas anyway. If the speech therapy were conducted in a center with other children whom your client could interact with, we could potentially take care of two issues at once, namely, the speech delay and socialization difficulties. If the child is around peers at this center, the parents, the speech therapist, and other child care professionals would be able to more closely observe the child to determine the level to which he interacts with peers.

In these types of situations, I will usually ask the parents to return with their child for a reevaluation after the child has received approximately three to six months of speech therapy from a Regional Center vendor. In this manner, there would potentially be a team of professionals or para-professionals who could provide me with additional information about the child's socialization around peers. We would also be able to learn how the child's language is developing with the addition of the speech therapy.

What about situations in which additional questions remain, such as does the child have a comorbid disorder? If you are evaluating a young child, are there concerns about other delays that need to be addressed? Would the child benefit from the administration of a more general developmental assessment, such as the Bayley Scales of Infant Development–Second Edition, the Gesell, or the Vineland Adaptive Behavior Scales? Maybe you are meeting an older child or a teenager, and there are questions about depression, intellectual functioning, or psychosis. If so, those assessments should be conducted as part of the thorough evaluation to determine if there are other factors that need to be taken into consideration.

Providing Feedback

If your evaluation is complete and all of your questions have been answered, not to mention both the parents'/caregiver's and the patient's questions, then it is time to discuss your findings. I have spoken with various professionals and parents who have mixed feelings about how feedback should be provided. One of the biggest issues that needs to be considered before even starting to provide feedback is one that is both very basic and very important: should the patient be in the room? I do not believe there are any hard-and-fast rules about how feedback should be given, with the exception that it be done in a caring and supportive manner. However, it would always be wise to ask the parents and/or the patient how they would like you to proceed. Needless to say, if the parent did not want to have the patient in the room when they were talking about the child's difficulties, they would most likely not want them in the room to discuss your findings.

Several years ago, an autism professional who has a son on the spectrum told me that when the family was going through all of the assessments decades ago, in an attempt to determine the cause of the child's difficulties, the child was in the room with the mother throughout the evaluation. She stated it was very difficult for her son to listen to all of her concerns, and as the evaluation progressed, he became sadder and more and more depressed. It obviously would have spared both the patient and the mother a great deal of sadness and grief if the history-gathering component of the evaluation were conducted without the child present.

My professional belief is that the patient should be present in the room when feedback is given. The reason for my preference is because the patient is the one we are talking about, and they should know the reason for the difficulties they are having. If you are evaluating a child, especially one moderately or severely affected by autism, it is quite likely they are not going to be at all interested in what is being discussed, which is also diagnostically relevant. However, with an individual who is less affected by autism, such as a teenager or an adult with Asperger's disorder or high-functioning autism, this information could be very helpful to them in more fully understanding why they do the things they do. If the patient or anyone else has strong feelings about not being in the room when feedback is given, I will always defer to them.

By having collected such a great deal of information about your client, you should have been able to determine if they have an ASD or any other type of disorder, for that matter. Assuming that the patient and/or the parents endorsed enough signs and symptoms to warrant a diagnosis of autism, there are a couple of ways to approach the topic.

First off, if the parents and the patient know specifically what you are looking for, namely, autism, it can be quite helpful to be upfront with them in a very respectful and professional manner. I might say something like "I've asked you all a great deal of questions about Johnny in order to get a better understanding of what your concerns are about him. By asking all of these questions about when Johnny was a little boy, I was able to get very specific information to help me determine if he is showing the symptoms necessary for a diagnosis of autism. We spoke a great deal about the three main problem areas for individuals with autism: socialization, language, and behavior. The information you told me [possibly combined with information they presented from other professionals, my observations of the child in my office, and whatever qualitative test measures I might have administered] supports a diagnosis of autism. Let me tell you how I came to that conclusion . . ." I then go through the information they imparted to me that is consistent with the diagnosis.

I don't like the idea of hemming and hawing around the topic of autism (well . . . I think . . . possibly . . . maybe . . .Johnny may have . . .I'm not sure . . .), nor profusely apologizing for coming up with a diagnosis (I feel really bad telling you this Mr. and Mrs. Smith and I am really sorry to let you know, but Johnny has autism). I don't believe that is the professional approach to the situation.

At that point, it is quite likely that the parents may have a rather strong reaction, one way or another, to the diagnosis. This reaction could range from them starting to cry out of depression, despair, or relief, being angry with you for being the bearer of bad news, or possibly feeling a tremendous weight off their shoulders because of the numerous times they thought something was wrong with their child and took them to various professionals, none of whom agreed with them or validated their feelings, until now.

I will then let the parents, the caregivers, and the patient ask all the questions they have, in order for them to best process the information they just received. As previously noted, sometimes the parents will be in shock and not have any questions. There may be times when a mother who has come to the evaluation without the father would tell you that the father will not agree with the diagnosis or that he is not going to want to hear it from her. At that time, I make a point of telling her that the label of autism is only important in that it provides an understanding of why her child does what he does, it does not change anything about him. The cute, funny, and quirky little boy who walked into my office two hours ago is still the same child, but now we simply have a much better understanding as to why he does the things he does and why he acts that way. With identifying the disorder also comes the understanding. We now know that Johnny has difficulty making and keeping friends because he has autism, not because he is difficult or oppositional or because his parents baby him too much. I also tell the mother that I will happily meet with her husband to tell him exactly how I came to this diagnosis, in such a way as to hopefully help him better accept it.

I have noticed that one of the main questions parents ask, which also appears to be one of the main issues that tends to upset the fathers, is the long-term prognosis of their child. As we are seeing more higher-functioning children these days, I typically tell the parents, as long as it is the truth, that while their child is currently having problems at the age of five, or ten, or whatever the child's age is at the time of the evaluation, if we get them services now at this young age, it would hopefully be less of an issue when they get older. Once you can help the parents get past the label of autism, which they may potentially view in the same vein as cancer, you can begin helping them to find ways to help their child.

I often tell parents that with this diagnosis, they now have a better sense of how to proceed. I often like to say to them, "If you were to have gone to the library yesterday to pick out a book to help you better understand your child, what would you have looked under? If you were to look up 'quirky children who are picky eaters who you thought could not hear when they were younger,' you probably would not have found anything. However, if you were to go to the library today and look up autism or Asperger's disorder, you would be presented with a great deal of very helpful information."

Assistance from the School

I let the parents know that we are now just beginning to take steps to improve their child's life by helping them get the services they need, such as speech therapy, social skills assistance, and possibly occupational therapy, through the school district. I inform the parents that I will write a report for them about our meeting, which they can take to the school in order to get an IEP for their child. The school should then ensure that the child is in the most appropriate classroom and gets appropriate services to help them to best access the academic curriculum.

I met the parents of a young woman in high school, who has been identified by both the Regional Center and the school district as having autism and mild mental retardation. When she was in junior high school, she was in a classroom with a caring and loving teacher who understood the best way to reach this student and help her to learn. Once she started high school, the environment changed completely, and she began soiling herself and assaulting both peers and teachers.

Instead of the school district taking a look at itself, trying to determine what had changed to cause this massive behavioral shift, and then taking steps to correct it, the girl's parents would simply be called and asked to come pick her up whenever she would engage in these behaviors. Instead of bringing in their trained professionals to assess the situation and help to find a way to correct it, they would ask the father (a truck driver) what should be done. Eventually, the school district expelled her from high school and had a teacher come to the family home three hours a week. This is a prime example of what school districts should not be doing for children with autism.

Simply bringing up special education can be another traumatizing factor for the parents. This may not be the case if the child also has cognitive limitations or a history of school difficulties. However, when you diagnose an intellectually gifted fourth grader with Asperger's disorder and suggest that the parents place him in special education, it can be a real shock for them. You will potentially need to educate the parents that special education is not only for children who function below grade level, but it is also for children with social skills deficits, language delays, and even gross motor, fine motor, or sensory integration issues.

I typically have to remind the parents that a diagnosis of autism or Asperger's disorder is not the same as mental retardation, but both require services from the school district. I tell the parents that some school districts have a very antiquated view of their role in the lives of children, namely, that they are there to teach them to read, write, and pass exit exams, nothing more. However, I do not believe that this is a very accurate view. I tell the parents that the main job of the school is to get children ready to be productive members of society. This entails helping them not only to acquire the math skills to run a register at the local supermarket when they are a teenager but also to have the appropriate social and pragmatic skills to shake the store manager's hand, look him or her in the eye, and ask for an application to work there. These social and pragmatic skills also need to fall under the purview of the school district, and those are the skills their intellectually gifted, but socially and linguistically delayed, child will learn through receiving special education services, whether in a pull-out setting or in a self-contained classroom.

I have also begun to tell parents that it is possible, if not likely, that when the school or the Regional Center does its own evaluation, it may not agree with my findings of autism, for whatever reason. I let the parents know that this is another example of it not being important what label is placed on their child by the school district, as long as they receive the appropriate services.

Some parents, like a surprising number of professionals, continue to have a more "classic" view of autism. They think of *Rain Man* or a child who bangs their head, flaps their arms, and never talks. A good percentage of the feedback time is spent educating the parents about the autism spectrum and how broad it is.

It has been my hope that by helping to educate professionals as to the broadness of the autism spectrum, the children, teens, and adults who do not fit the classic pattern of autism will no longer be overlooked.

Appendix A

Sample Copy of My Questionnaire

Name:_____

Date:_____

AUTISM SPECTRUM DISORDERS DIAGNOSTIC INTERVIEW

When did you first become concerned about your child?

_____
_____
_____
_____
_____
_____
_____
_____
_____

What services is the child receiving or has received?

_____
_____
_____
_____

Prenatal, perinatal, and postnatal history:

_____

_____

_____

_____

_____

Problems or complications with pregnancy?

_____

Born on time?

_____

Healthy at birth?

_____

Weight and length:

_____

Medical history:

_____

_____

_____

_____

_____

_____

Has the child had a hearing test?

_____

Does he point?

_____

Developmental milestones (crawling, walking, toilet training, etc.):

_____

Toilet trained:

_____

_____

Motor skills (clumsy)?

_____

_____

How does the child behave at parties?

_____

_____

_____

_____

_____

_____

1. Problems in social interaction

a: Difficulty with non-verbal behaviors such as eye contact, body posture, and gestures in social relationships:

_____

_____

Does he look at you when you call his name?

_____

b: Any age appropriate friends?

_____

_____

_____

_____

c: Does he show, bring, or point out things to you that interest him?

_____

d: Does he reciprocate the things you do for him, or does he do things for you?

_____

2. Problems with communication

a: Does he speak? If so, was it delayed? Does he attempt to compensate through gestures or mime?

_____

Has he lost or forgotten any words, or has there been any regression in his language?

_____

b: If his speech is OK, does he have problems starting or sustaining conversations?

_____

_____

c: Does he have **a repetitive** or strange use of language (such as flipping pronouns, echolalia, having very literal understanding of the world, speaking in a robotic or monotone voice, or acting like a "little professor")?

_____

_____

_____

_____

Does he recite lines from movies or television shows?

_____

d: Does he engage in spontaneous make-believe play that is appropriate to his developmental level?

_____

_____

Does he pursue only one topic regardless of the conversation?

_____

_____

_____

3. Repetitive and stereotyped patterns of behaviors, interests and activities

a: Preoccupation with one or more things (for example, bus schedule, astronomy):

_____

_____

_____

b: Problems with change: Does he have to stay with a particular routine?

_____

_____

c: Any repetitive movements such as hand or finger flapping?

_____

If so, when do they occur and can they be interrupted?

_____

_____

d: Intense interest in parts of objects (staring intensely at lights or textured objects):

_____

4. Play

a: Can the child use play materials in an imaginative way?

_____

b: Does he become preoccupied by unusual aspects of play materials, such as the feel or the sound?

_____

_____

_____

_____

c: Is the play repetitive and stereotyped in nature?

_____

d: How does he react when you hold him?

_____

e: As an infant and a toddler, did he like physical closeness and affection?

_____

f: How would he react when you would leave him at the age of about seven to eight months?

_____

g: Would he wander away from you and not care?

_____

_____

h: Is he overly sensitive to sounds, smells, clothes, and the like?

_____

_____

i: Any problems with eating?

_____

j: Does he play with toys appropriately?

_____

k: Does he line up his toys or arrange them by color or shape?

_____

l: How was his eye contact with me?

_____

m: Did he imitate as a youngster?

_____

n: How is his pain tolerance?

_____

o: Behavioral observations:

_____
_____
_____
_____
_____
_____
_____

Appendix B

Sample Copies of Reports

I am including several reports as a way of showing how I incorporate all of the information I obtain into a cohesive whole.

Report 1: David, Age 3

In my evaluation of this patient, I did not utilize either the ADOS (Autism Diagnostic Observation Schedule) or the ADI-R (Autism Diagnostic Interview—Revised) for a couple of reasons. First and foremost is that my observations of David during our time together showed very definitive signs of autism, which would clearly be scored as problematic on the ADOS. Why keep this unhappy, head-banging child in my office for an additional hour when I have already seen and the mother has already described the behaviors that are suggestive of autism? Second, in my two hours with the mother and David, mother endorsed more than enough signs to warrant a diagnosis. The benefit that could have been obtained by spending another three hours with the mother administering the ADI-R did not seem worth the additional time it would take to acquire the information.

Consultation Report of the Department of Behavioral Medicine

ASD Diagnostic Service

Reason for Consultation
An evaluation was requested to rule out an ASD. At the age of 14 months, David was seen by an occupational therapist because of his oral tactile defensiveness. Two months later, his social and language skills were reported to have declined. David currently has an expressive vocabulary of 50–60 words and bangs his head against the wall on a fairly regular basis.

Consultation History
David is being seen by a psychologist in the community to assist with his socialization and language delays. The mother expressed concern about these areas of David's development. The mother noted that David bangs his head when he gets mad or when he does not get what he wants.

On May 4, 2004, David was evaluated by the Fresno County Unified School District's Preschool Assessment Team. That evaluation found David to be displaying several autistic-like behaviors, such as "an inability to use language for appropriate communication, a history of withdrawal and inappropriate social interaction in relating [sic] to people other than his immediate family and self-stimulating ritualistic behaviors." David was also administered the Developmental Profile II, which found him to have a 25%–50% delay in the areas of communication, cognition, and social and emotional development.

David is also being seen by a speech therapist twice a week. The mother reported that David's vocabulary is improving. On November 18, 2004, he had a speech and language evaluation, which revealed a moderate-to-severe delay in both the receptive and the expressive language. It was further noted that David showed weakness in regard to his behavioral compliance, attention, and imitation skills. The speech therapist went on to state, "It is unclear as to what may be the cause of these difficulties; however, they may appear to be the result of an underlying social communication disorder." A recommendation was made for David to be seen by a child psychologist or developmental pediatrician to rule out autism.

Prenatal and Perinatal History
David was born full term, following an emergency Cesarean section secondary to fetal distress. The mother was in labor for 17 hours, and David's heart rate had dropped. It was reported that the umbilical cord was wrapped around

David's neck twice. No additional complications were noted, and David did not require oxygen or ventilation. He was born mildly jaundiced and required some light therapy. At the time of birth, David weighed 7 pounds, 3 ounces and was 20 inches long.

Medical History

With the exception of three or four ear infections during the first year of his life, David is a healthy young boy who does not have a history of major medical problems, such as illnesses, injuries, broken bones, surgeries, seizures, or hospitalizations. The parents recently attempted to assess David's hearing through the use of headphones, but he was unresponsive. His hearing is due to be rechecked next week.

Developmental History

David rolled over "late," sat on his own at the age of seven months, crawled at the age of eight months, and walked at the age of 12 months. He first cooed on time, said "mama" and "dada" at the age of 12 months, and started naming objects at the age of 2 $\frac{1}{2}$ years. David occasionally points to what he wants. He also has a history of using sign language and taking his mother's hand and putting it on what he wants. Gross motor coordination does not appear to be a problem for David. The mother noted that David is almost potty trained.

Behavioral Observations

David's evaluation lasted for approximately two hours and included his mother and the case coordinator. During our time together, David would not interact with any of the adults in the room, despite numerous attempts. David also did not play with any of the examiner's toys, such as cars, blocks, balls, or crayons. Instead, David walked over to the phone and held it to his ear. He would then drop the phone, pick it up, and drop it again. This behavior happened repeatedly. David would often flip the light switches off and on and even sat in the trashcan in the examination room. There were several times when David banged his head, full force, into the wall. He did not appear at all phased or hurt by having done so.

While there were times when David banged his head if he was not given what he wanted, there were other times when he would bang his head for reasons unknown to the adults in the room. Toward the end of our time together, David turned over his stroller and spun the wheels for 15 minutes.

Assessment Findings and Impressions

David is showing several, significant signs of autism, as he is displaying difficulties in all areas consistent with the disorder, namely, problems with social interaction, communication and stereotyped patterns of behaviors and interests.

David's mother noted that he makes sporadic eye contact with others and only occasionally looks at people when they call his name. She went on to say that David is very happy "doing his own thing" but will occasionally bring toys to his parents to play with. The examiner was unable to determine if David brings things to his parents in order for them to serve some type of purpose or if David truly wants to interact with them. The mother also stated David watches other children when they are running around but loses interest in what they are doing when they stop engaging in physical play. It was further noted that David points at animals and then looks at his parents, but there is not much additional pointing or showing. David does not bring or give objects to others.

In the realm of communication, David's language development was delayed, and he has a vocabulary of only 50–60 words. David is also showing some of the stereotyped patterns of behaviors and interests common in children with autism. For example, even though he is only three years old, his mother noted that he loves to play Halo on the X-Box, and there are times when he carries a stick or some other object around with him for the entire day. David does not have difficulty coping with changes to his routine but grinds his teeth and bangs his head often.

As an infant and a toddler, David liked to be picked up and held. When he was less than one year old, at the prime separation anxiety stage, David would become appropriately upset when his mother or other primary caretaker would leave his line of sight. David has a history of wandering away from his parents, but the mother noted that he looks back to see where she is. She went on to say that David is oblivious to his surroundings and may not be aware of the dangers around him.

David is not displaying any sensory integration issues, with the exception of being a very picky eater. He actually stopped eating at the age of 15 months and would only drink milk. There were also times when he would only eat McDonald's chicken nuggets, not nuggets from the grocery store. He will also not drink out of a cup. David usually plays with his toys appropriately and does not line them up or arrange them by color or shape. He occasionally imitates and wants to do the things that his parents do, such as pretending to cook or clean.

Treatment Plan
The mother was informed of this examiner's conclusion that David has autism, *DSM-IV-TR* code 299.00. He is in need of (and will hopefully be found eligible for) services from the school district and the Regional Center. It would be helpful for him to be placed in an appropriate educational setting in which he

can readily access the academic curriculum, such as an autistic classroom in a regular education school or a nonpublic school that specializes in teaching children with autism. Given the destructive nature of David's head banging, it is crucial that his school placement be in a facility in which the staff is trained to deal with such behavior.

The mother was provided with resources about autism, both within and outside of her healthcare plan.

Report 2: Ralph, Age 3

As in David's case, from Report 1, Ralph is also three years old, and the ADOS and the ADI-R were not utilized in his assessment either. However, this was a child whom I did not diagnosis with autism. The primary reason why I did not use the ADOS with Ralph was because the information I obtained from the parents, which was quite consistent with Ralph's presentation during our time together, only noted minor socialization difficulties and none of the behavioral difficulties required for a diagnosis.

Given that the history provided by the parents was not consistent with a diagnosis of autism, administering an ADOS to this child would probably not have provided any additional information. For example, if I administered the ADOS to Ralph and he did not display the social or linguistic problems consistent with autism (just as the parents had reported), there would not be any elevations on the ADOS, which would further support what the parents had told me. If there were elevations on the ADOS that could be suggestive of autism, there still would not be the history necessary for a diagnosis as reported by the parents. As the ADOS is a classification and not a diagnostic tool, just having scores in the autistic range on the ADOS does not mean the patient merits a diagnosis.

Consultation Report of the Department of Behavioral Medicine

ASD Diagnostic Service

Reason for Consultation
An evaluation was requested to rule out an ASD because of language delays and a rather atypical presentation.

Consultation History

Ralph's parents noted that his preschool teacher has concerns about his short attention span, interest in toy trains, and speech delay. The parents reported only being concerned about his speech delay. Ralph has been enrolled in preschool for the past two years and is quite happy there.

Last December, Ralph had a speech and language evaluation that found his listening comprehension and expressive language skills to be below his age level. Ralph was also seen by a speech therapist. The parents have contacted the Ventura County Unified School District to begin the process of obtaining an IEP for Ralph to provide him with school-based speech therapy.

Prenatal and Perinatal History

The mother noted that her pregnancy and delivery were normal and without any problem or complication. Ralph was born two weeks late and healthy, weighing 7 pounds, 4 ounces and was 21 inches long.

Medical History

The parents noted that Ralph has a history of colds and ear infections. Ralph also had stitches on his lip after falling and cutting his lip. Ralph's hearing was assessed last month and was found to be fine.

Developmental History

Ralph achieved his motor milestones on time. The parents noted that he cooed and babbled on time. Ralph spoke his first word "dada" at the age of 13 months. Gross and fine motor coordination is not a problem for Ralph. He is not yet toilet trained.

Behavioral Observations

Ralph's evaluation lasted for two hours and included his parents and the case coordinator. During our time together, Ralph threw a ball around the room, even after being repeatedly told not to do so. He was also quite loud throughout the evaluation. Ralph's play skills, as shown during the evaluation, were quite underdeveloped, as he would play with the toy cars by taking them out of the container, label them, and put them back. His eye contact was sporadic, and he became rather upset toward the end of the evaluation, something the parents attributed to hunger.

Assessment Findings and Impressions

Ralph's parents did not endorse enough signs or symptoms to suggest an ASD, as he is not displaying difficulty with social interactions or stereotyped patterns of behaviors and interests.

Ralph's parents noted that he only makes brief eye contact with others but looks at people when they call his name. They also believe that Ralph is able to understand their nonverbal behavior and body language. The parents went on to say that Ralph loves the children who live next door and often asks to play with them. The vast majority of the time when Ralph plays with others, no problems arise. He spends his time with other children, engaging in socially appropriate interchanges. When Ralph is taken to the park, he is very interested in what the other children are doing and wants to interact with them. However, he tends to have poor body boundaries and gets right up in their faces. When he is taken to birthday parties, Ralph is also appropriately social. He often shows and brings things to others that interest him and typically does nice things for others, such as picking a flower for his mother and giving it to her and drawing things and giving it to his parents and teachers.

In the realm of communication, as previously noted by the speech pathologist, Ralph's speech skills are below his age level. Ralph is not showing any of the stereotyped patterns of behaviors or interests common in children with autism. For example, he does not have any preoccupation with anything, has minimal difficulty coping with changes to his routine when he has some warning, typically does not engage in repetitive hand or body movements, and does not have an intense interest in parts or pieces of things.

As an infant and a toddler, Ralph was fine being picked up and held. When he was less than one year old, at the prime separation anxiety stage, Ralph would not be upset when his mother or other primary caretaker would leave his line of sight. Ralph does not have a history of wandering away from his parents.

Ralph is not displaying any sensory integration issues and is not a picky eater. Ralph plays with toys appropriately and in creative ways and does not line them up or arrange them by color or shape. He only occasionally imitates or wants to do the things his parents do, such as pretending to cook or clean.

Treatment Plan
Ralph is not displaying enough signs and symptoms to be consistent with having an ASD. It is recommended that he be referred for an occupational therapy and sensory integration evaluation. Ralph would also benefit from continued speech therapy. If satisfactory progress is not made in the next six months, it is recommended that Ralph return to be reevaluated.

Report 3: John, Age 17

After providing examples of evaluations with children, one of whom was diagnosed with autism, John is an example of a teenager whom I saw for an evaluation and with whom I utilized both the ADI-R and the ADOS. While I had already seen John years earlier and diagnosed him with autism without the use of these two instruments, I used both measures this time to provide the family with quantifiable evidence of John's diagnosis to present to the Regional Center and school district.

Consultation Report of the Department of Behavioral Medicine

ASD Diagnostic Service

Reason for Consultation
An evaluation was requested to confirm a previous diagnosis of autism.

Consultation History
John began preschool at the age of four and appeared to do well. However, he would often play by himself and did not make any friends. During the second year of preschool, John's teachers noted that he continued to be a loner, had difficulty sitting still during quiet time, and was very disruptive. A note from John's kindergarten teacher asked to have him evaluated because of his inability to perform and function in the kindergarten classroom. The following year, a note from John's first-grade teacher noted that he was working below grade level in all academic areas.

In 1995, John was seen by a child psychiatrist who diagnosed him with the combined type of ADHD and prescribed Ritalin. A report from the school psychologist, dated October 1999, noted, "John has shown measurable cognitive loss in his nonverbal ability since last psychological testing two years ago and his academic achievement continues to lag significantly below that of his peers. The ADHD symptomatology has not lessened during this period in addition. Present test results and behavior observation indicate a processing deficit in attention, accounting for a severe ability–achievement discrepancy in mathematics. It is recommended that the RSP services continue."

A note from one of John's teachers, dated June 2000, stated that while John is well behaved, he "seems to have very little interaction with his peers. He seems to prefer to keep to himself a great deal." In May 2003, John was found to be eligible for speech and language and hard-of-hearing services as a child with an Other Health Impairment, Language- and Speech-Specific Learning Disability, and Deafness and Hearing.

In 2004, John was seen by an adolescent therapist because of mother's wish for him to be more social. It was noted that John did not share his mother's concerns about his socializing and preferred to focus on doing better in school. It was also around this time that John's IEP found him to be eligible for services as a student who is hard of hearing and has speech and language impairment. As a result, John was placed in a resource class for math and English, in addition to receiving speech therapy, which he had been receiving for quite some time.

In December of 2004, John was diagnosed with autism by this examiner. The following year, John was seen by a Regional Center psychologist for an evaluation. At that time, he was found to have average intellectual ability, as determined by the Leiter International Performance–Revised. On the Wide Range Achievement Test, Third Edition, John was functioning at the seventh-grade level for reading recognition and the fifth-grade level for arithmetic. On the Vineland Adaptive Behavior Scales, with the mother as the respondent, John had a scaled score of 79 in communication, 60 in daily living skills, and 65 on socialization skills. The psychologist then diagnosed John with PDD-NOS.

On John's latest IEP, dated June 2006, it was noted he was "apathetic towards class and the teacher. His class work assignments are incomplete but he tries. His homework is also incomplete . . . He needs to improve his attention." John was found eligible for only speech and language therapy in the area of pragmatics. At that time, the IEP team agreed that a formal assessment to determine if John has autism was warranted.

Prenatal and Perinatal History
The mother noted her pregnancy and delivery were uneventful. John was born healthy and on time, weighing 7 pounds, 12 ounces and was 19 inches long.

Medical History
Beginning at the age of 12 months, John began to develop frequent ear infections. Because of these ear infections, John had tubes placed in his ears twice, and his tonsils and adenoids were removed at the age of four. After that time, it was noted that John made remarkable improvements in both speech and hearing.

Developmental History
The mother noted that John rolled over at the age of four months, sat up at the age of nine months, crawled at the age of 10 months, and walked at the age of 11 months. He reportedly cooed and said "mama" and "dada" at the age of 12 months. He said his first word "ball" between the ages of 12 and 13 months. The mother stated that there may have been a slight hearing loss at the age of four, but it has gotten worse in the past few years. Toilet training was very difficult for John, as he had accidents constantly at preschool, with both urination and defecation until the age of six or seven. Gross motor coordination is not a problem for John.

Behavioral Observations
John's evaluation lasted for approximately four hours over a two-day period. At the time of our first meeting, the mother was administered the ADI-R. At the time of our second meeting, John was administered module 4 of the ADOS. John's behavior during our time together is noted in the ADOS section.

Assessment Findings and Impressions
Autism Diagnostic Interview—Revised (ADI-R)

	Obtained Scores	Cutoff Scores
Qualitative impairments in social interaction	24	10
Communication	18	8
Repetitive behaviors and stereotyped patterns	9	3
Abnormality of development evident at or before 36 months	3	1

The ADI-R is a structured, standardized assessment of communication, social interaction, and behavior for individuals where an ASD is suspected. Scores at or above the cutoff indicate a higher likelihood of an ASD.

The following table provides the raw score tallies that were totaled to acquire the above-listed "obtained score." Higher scores reflect a combination of autistic-type characteristics and their severity. Ratings are based on both the patient's current behavior and their behavior in childhood (at the age of four to five years) as specified by the ADI-R directions.

Score	Qualitative Impairments in Reciprocal Social Interaction
2	1. John would look at people when speaking to them but only for short periods of time and not on a consistent basis. John would also smile occasionally when looking at others. As a child, John displayed a full range of facial expressions toward others.
8	2. When John was younger, he would be much more interested in watching other children play than interacting with them. When he would interact, John would engage in only physical play with others, not any type of pretend play. If other children whom John knew would approach him, he would rarely show any interest in interacting with them. John did not have any friends when he was younger whom he would ask to see outside of school.
6	3. While John would show and bring things to his parents when he was younger, it would be either objects related to his intense preoccupation with something and or him requiring assistance with something. John would also never share, without being asked to do so. He would also not attempt to share his excitement about something with his parents or other individuals.

8

4. When John was a child, he would occasionally place his parent's hands on something he wanted or would use their hands like a tool. He would rarely attempt to comfort others if they were sad or upset. John would also display facial expressions that were inconsistent with his situation, and he would often have rather inappropriate responses to others.

Score
7
6
4
1

Qualitative Impairments in Communication

1. John made only few attempts as a child to direct his parent's attention to objects or activities that interested him. He would also neither nod nor shake his head to gesture "yes" or "no." However, John would use more typical gestures, such as waving good-bye.

2. John would only spontaneously imitate a very limited number of actions as a child and would not engage in any creative, imaginative play or social play.

3. John would typically only talk to others to get a need met, not to socialize with them. He also had a history of tremendous difficulty sustaining back-and-forth conversations with others.

4. John's speech patterns tended to be more repetitive than other children, but he does not have a history of asking any inappropriate questions, flipping his pronouns, or making up words.

Score
3
4
0
2

Repetitive Behaviors and Stereotyped Patterns

1. John has a history of intense preoccupations, which has intruded upon his family's life, as well as hobbies that he is more interested in than would be considered typical.

2. John has a history of engaging in verbal rituals to such an extent that they have intruded into and interfered with his family life. There are also activities John has to engage in to a significant degree. If he is not allowed to or prevented from doing so, John will feel extreme anxiety and stress.

3. John does not have a history of any repetitive hand or finger mannerism, nor any complicated body movements.

4. John's play as a child was highly stereotyped and involved him playing with toys in an atypical manner. However, he does not have a history of any intense sensory interest, such as needing to touch, taste, smell, or hold objects or toys.

Autism Diagnostic Observation Schedule (ADOS) Module 4
The ADOS is a semi-structured, standardized assessment of communication, social interaction, and play for individuals who have been referred because of possible autism or other pervasive developmental disorders. Administration consists of a series of planned social occasions or "presses" in which a behavior of a particular type is likely to occur. Across the session the examiner presents numerous opportunities for the individual being assessed to exhibit behaviors of interest in the diagnostic process. A module chosen to be appropriate to a

Area	Obtained Score	ADOS Algorithm Cutoff	
		Autism Spectrum	Autism
Communication	5	2	3
Reciprocal social interaction	12	4	6
Stereotyped behaviors and restricted interests	0	*No cutoffs determined*	
Imagination/creativity	1	*No cutoffs determined*	
Communication and social interaction total	17	7	10

particular language level dictates the protocol. At the end of the administration, ratings are completed based on the observation period. The obtained scores are compared with the ADOS cutoff scores to assist in diagnosis. Scores at or above the cutoff indicate a higher likelihood of an ASD.

For this assessment all of the required items from module 4 were administered. Module 4 is appropriate for an adolescent or an adult who has fluent speech. The descriptions provided below involve only those behaviors and clinical impressions that are needed to ascertain the presence of autistic traits.

Language and Communication: John used sentences in a correct fashion and did not engage in any echolalia, either immediate or delayed. He also did not use any stereotyped or odd words and phrases. However, there was little variation in the tone and pitch of his speech; he never offered any information spontaneously to the examiner, never asked the examiner about his thoughts or feelings, only reported events when prompted to do so, and was unable to sustain any type of conversation. John also engaged in only a limited number of gestures.

Reciprocal Social Interaction: John displayed poorly modulated eye contact, did not direct much facial expression toward the examiner, did not show any insight into typical social situations, and displayed only limited understanding of others' emotions. John showed limited understanding of his own level of responsibility, made negligible social overtures to the examiner, and did not engage in reciprocal social communication with the examiner.

Stereotyped Behaviors/Restricted Interests: No unusual sensory interests, hand/finger movements or other complex mannerisms, or compulsions or rituals were observed during the ADOS.

Imagination/Creativity: While John did engage in some creative or make-believe actions, they were rather limited in range.

Other Abnormal Behaviors: John displayed some mild signs of anxiety throughout the evaluation.

Treatment Plan
The information obtained on both the ADOS and the ADI-R supports John's previous diagnosis of autism. Given this fact, he is in continued need of services from both the Regional Center and the school district to help him to lead as full and as complete a life as possible. It is quite likely that John will require some vocational training to help him become successful in whatever job he undertakes in the future.

Report 4: Sam, Age 31

Sam is a young man who came to see me, never having been diagnosed with autism. His parents' desire in seeking an evaluation was for Sam to be able to receive ongoing services from the Regional Center, which would help him in obtaining steady employment and the ability to live outside of the home, without his parents' continued and consistent assistance.

Because of the need to provide a very strong case for Sam having a diagnosis of autism, he was administered the ADOS and the parents were interviewed utilizing both the Vineland Adaptive Behavior Scales–Second Edition (VABS II) and the ADI-R, in addition to my standard, in-depth interview.

Consultation Report of the Department of Behavioral Medicine

ASD Diagnostic Service

Reason for Consultation
An evaluation was requested to determine if Sam has an ASD.

Procedures Administered
The ADOS module 4, the VABS-II, and the ADI-R along with a clinical interview with the parents and the patient were conducted.

Consultation History

In elementary school, Sam was uncomfortable being around peers, as he felt like an outsider and did not know what to do when he was around others. While Sam did have a few friends in the neighborhood around this time, he would only play with them for a short period of time before wanting to be alone.

In middle school, Sam enjoyed archery and was progressing well. When he was informed that continued archery lessons would include him teaching other students, Sam suddenly dropped the sport and never took it up again. While in middle school, Sam would spend his free time as well as mealtimes alone, as he preferred to be in the library, where he would not stand out. Sam felt very awkward in high school and did not have any peers whom he would see outside of school. In high school, Sam played golf and ran marathons but never developed any friendship playing those sports. It was around this time that Sam started to become more sullen and withdrawn. His parents noted that he was frustrated by his difficulties, both within and outside of school.

At the age of 16, Sam underwent a speech and language evaluation through the Clovis Unified School District because of his difficulty in processing spoken information. Sam's receptive language was found to be two standard deviations above the mean, while he was noted to have difficulty with pragmatics and the ability to carry on a back-and-forth conversation.

In 1995, Sam graduated from high school with relatively poor grades. He then enrolled at a local community college before dropping out in his first year. In the spring of 1996, Sam started working at Trader Joe's Supermarket. While there, Sam was unable to work the cash register and was uncomfortable interacting with customers. Sam was also unable to develop any true relationship with his coworkers and never met any of them outside of work. It was around this time that Sam had a blind date with the sister of a fellow employee, which reportedly did not go well. That was Sam's first and last date.

One year later, Sam was briefly employed at a local department store, where his significant interpersonal difficulties continued. One of Sam's pleasures at work was to watch the sink fill up with water before letting it drain. There were reportedly several instances when Sam would become distracted and have to clean up the mess when the sink overflowed. When Sam began jumping up and down on packing material in an attempt to make his coworkers laugh, the manager fired him on the spot, walked him to his car, and told him never to come back.

From June 1997, for a few months, Sam worked part time at a local pet store, taking care of the animals. After his supervisor left the company and Sam began working alone, he became extremely disorganized, and his high level of anxiety prevented him from working effectively. Sam's ability to work decreased dramatically, and he began arriving for work several hours late. After months of this behavior, Sam's employer called his parents to ask if their son "had any mental disability."

In the last few years of his employment, Sam required between 10 and 12 hours a day to complete four hours of work. Sam was not paid for any time he spent at work after the initial four hours. Sam was soon overwhelmed by what he viewed as an "unmanageable" amount of work and being over-tasked by his employer. It was not until Sam told his therapist how overwhelmed he was that he finally decided to quit his job.

Sam is currently unemployed and continues to live with his parents. The parents believe Sam is very self-conscious and overly sensitive to criticism. Sam was noted to be uncomfortable being himself around others and feels he needs to be careful about what he says.

A few years ago, Sam underwent a psychoeducational assessment to assist him with his career planning. The evaluation found Sam to have a verbal IQ score of 115 and a performance IQ of 84. This 31-point verbal–performance split is highly unusual and clinically significant. This type of nonverbal learning disability is quite common among individuals on the autism spectrum.

The assessor went on to note that Sam has a very literal interpretation of spoken language and "slow or no response to puns, idioms, and sarcasm. Social pragmatic difficulties were notable for deficits in nonverbal language, including rare use of gestures, body movement or facial expression to convey ideas, and little change in voice tone or quality." Sam was also noted to lack friends and has never had a best friend. It was reported that Sam wants to have friends and to learn how to interact with others his age. In the conclusion of the report, it was noted, "Sam is depressed with his inability to make friends in spite of the desire to do so. He is not yet able to live independently."

Sam enjoys golf and has done so for approximately 10 years. In all that time, Sam has not made any friends. He does not like to participate in team sports, as he does not like to assert himself. Sam now spends a great deal of time watching television and doing chores around the house. In fact, Sam spends an inordinate amount of time engaging in typical household activities. The parents noted that cleaning his dishes and putting them in the dishwasher, something which would take them less than a minute to do, requires 10–20 times as long for Sam, as he will don his gloves and undertake a meticulous routine that cannot be deviated from. There have been times when Sam would not go out of the house, as he needed to spend more than an hour organizing his clothes or going through every item in the refrigerator to check the expiration date.

In the recent past, Sam has been attending a support group for individuals with autism and Asperger's disorder, led by two graduate students. Sam has struggled for so long with his insecurities and inability to understand what to do in various situations that he is overwhelmed by a sense of low self-esteem and social adjustments difficulties. There have also been instances in the past when Sam would become frustrated and punch holes in walls and doors.

It was further noted that Sam "barely understands the basics of income, money management, and expenditures." When he was working, Sam would typically toss his paycheck into a drawer and forget about it. It was only after his parents pestered him that Sam would make a deposit. There were also times when Sam would deposit as many as 10 checks at once. Sam typically has no idea how much money he has in the bank, nor how to pay his bills.

Prenatal and Perinatal History
Sam was born healthy and on time. The mother did not note any problem or complication with her pregnancy.

Medical History
As a young child, Sam was in the hospital frequently. As a teenager and now as an adult, Sam has been very healthy. For about the past year, Sam has been taking medication to help with his depression.

Developmental History
At the age of two, Sam underwent a developmental evaluation. His motor and language skills were delayed by 10 months. His adaptive skills were delayed by eight months, and his personal/social skills were delayed by 13 months. Sam was toilet trained at the age of five.

Behavioral Observations
The vast majority of my evaluation consisted of meeting Sam's parents for the administration of the Vineland, the ADI-R, and the clinical interview. During my two-hour meeting with Sam, his eye contact was quite inconsistent, and he often spoke in a very flat and monotone voice. A high level of anxiety was also noted from the very beginning of our meeting. During the ADOS, Sam would often ask me if he was doing all right or if he had done something correctly. Sam would often talk at tremendous lengths while staring at the wall about topics that were only somewhat related to what was being discussed in the evaluation. During our time together, Sam reported, "I have not had a lot of success in my life with neurotypicals."

Assessment Findings and Impressions
Sam has a lifelong history and has been significantly affected by all of the signs of autism, *DSM-IV-TR* code 299.00. He is displaying difficulties in the areas consistent with the disorder, namely, problems with social interaction, communication and stereotyped patterns of behaviors and interests.

Sam has a significant history of socialization difficulties. His eye contact has always been poor, and he rarely responds to or looks at someone when they call his name. This is the case whether it is his parents, other family members, or strangers trying to get his attention. Sam is also basically unable to understand nonverbal communication and body language. If he is talking incessantly about one of his many topics of interest, he is unable to discern that others are not interested in hearing what he is talking about.

As a young child, Sam was very content to play alone in his room for prolonged periods of time. In fact, Sam has always had difficulty playing appropriately with others. When the mother would set up play dates for Sam in preschool, he would come crying to her that the other children were too loud or were messing up his room. The mother noted that Sam was clearly distressed at having other children in his personal space. As a child, Sam also would not ask to see others and did not want to go over to other people's homes.

Sam typically does not like to watch plays or dramas on television, as he is unable to form any type of emotional connection with the characters or the plot. He also actively avoids interactions with neighbors, although he may call them to see if he could play with their pets. As a child, Sam would not know how to go about meeting people or what to do or say to "break the ice." As a result, Sam began asking people, " Do you like trains?" When his parents informed Sam that this was not an appropriate question, Sam switched to asking them if they like apples, which he continues to do to this day.

In terms of the communication difficulties common among individuals with autism, Sam spoke in a singsong cadence as a child. As he grew older, his facial expression and tone of voice grew flat. Now, Sam speaks in a very flat tone of voice, with no facial expressions, gestures, or body language. Sam has also always been a very black-and-white thinker and has significant difficulty in coping with concepts and answers to questions that do not fit into those categories. The pragmatics of conversation is also an area of difficulty for Sam and is something he rarely does. As Sam does not view "small talk" as genuine, he will not engage in those pleasantries and therefore appears rude or aloof at times. However, there was an instance when Sam was 13 and walked into his sister's room, to chat with her. Unfortunately, it was 2 AM at the time. Sam's understanding of sarcasm, jokes, and idioms is also very limited.

In regard to the stereotyped and repetitive manners common among individuals with autism, Sam has developed very rigid and self-imposed standards. Once this overly elaborate, overly complex, and truly time-consuming routine is put into place, Sam has significant difficulty deviating from it. The parents noted that Sam requires a great deal of "sameness and predictability" and fights against change. For example, Sam is reported to engage in a 90-minute bathroom routine, which cannot be changed or expedited. This typically results in Sam being late for almost every appointment or engagement he has. There have been instances in which Sam has been unable to get out of the house because he is so focused on his to-do list.

Sam is typically unable to make it to appointments on time or get to a store before it closes because of the length of time it takes him to complete a task. Other changes to routines such as making coffee, preparing to drive somewhere, or having houseguests are all activities that can cause Sam significant unease if specific routines are not followed.

When he was younger, Sam was obsessed with traffic lights and the Loch Ness Monster. He would then talk at people about these subjects for prolonged periods of time. Sam also has a history of rocking back and forth as a child. As a young child, Sam never engaged in creative or imaginative play. He would not interact with his brother directly and mainly engaged in parallel play.

Sam is also displaying several signs of a sensory integration disorder, as his parents noted that he does not like loud noises and was terrified of fireworks as a child. He also did not like to be picked up or held and did not want anybody to rub his neck or back.

Autism Diagnostic Interview—Revised (ADI-R)

	Obtained Scores	Cutoff Scores
Qualitative impairments in social interaction	26	10
Communication	22	8
Repetitive behaviors and stereotyped patterns	9	3
Abnormality of development evident at or before 36 months	1	1

The ADI-R is a structured, standardized assessment of communication, social interaction, and behavior for individuals where an ASD is suspected. Scores at or above the cutoff indicate a higher likelihood of an ASD.

The following table provides the raw score tallies that were totaled to acquire the obtained score.

Score	Qualitative Impairments in Reciprocal Social Interaction
5	1. Sam has a history of inconsistent eye contact and generally would not engage in social smiling as a child. Sam also displayed a markedly limited range of facial expressions as a child.
7	2. While Sam would occasionally play with others as a child, he did not engage in any pretend play. He would rarely approach others and would be unpredictable in his response to other children when they approached him. Sam did enjoy some parallel play with other children but little or no cooperative play. When Sam was in the middle and high schools, he did not have any peer relationships which involved sharing.

| 6 | 3. Sam would bring things to others when he was a child, but it was typically restricted to his intense preoccupations, food, or a need for help. Sam would only share items with others as a child when instructed to do so. |
| 8 | 4. Sam would occasionally place another person's hand on objects or use the other person's hand as if it were a tool. He would rarely offer comfort to others when they were in distress and would infrequently use a combination of eye contact and vocalization to get his needs met. Sam's facial expressions were usually not appropriate to the situation, and he would respond to others in a very limited manner. |

Score	Qualitative Impairments in Communication
8	1. As a child, Sam made little or no attempt to bring his parents' attention to things that interested him. He also never nodded or shook his head spontaneously. Sam would only inconsistently use gestures.
6	2. As a child, Sam would only spontaneously imitate a limited number of activities his parents would engage in and would only occasionally engage in pretend play. When others would engage in this sort of play, it was typically not reciprocated by Sam.
4	3. Sam would rarely speak to others as a child for purely social reasons. He would typically speak only to get a need met. Sam continues to have tremendous difficulty in maintaining reciprocal conversations.
4	4. Sam has a history of stereotyped utterances and a continued, frequent use of odd questions and statements.

Score	Repetitive Behaviors and Stereotyped Patterns
2	1. While Sam does not have a history of unusual preoccupations, he becomes fixated on specific hobbies and interests.
3	2. Sam used to have a tendency to say things in a specific manner and make his parents do the same. These rituals continue to intrude upon family life and cause problems if interrupted. There are also certain compulsions and rituals that Sam continues to engage in, which take up a prolonged period of time and will cause significant intrafamilial conflict if disrupted.
2	3. Sam does not have a history of any hand or finger mannerism but does engage in complex body movements, such as spinning, walking on his tiptoes, and running with an awkward gait.
2	4. As a child, Sam's play was highly stereotyped, as he was more interested in examining a toy than playing with it in the manner in which it was created.

Autism Diagnostic Observation Schedule (ADOS Module 4)

The ADOS is a semi-structured, standardized assessment of communication, social interaction and play for individuals who have been referred because of possible autism or other pervasive developmental disorders. Administration consists of a series of planned social occasions or "presses" in which a behavior

Area	Obtained Score	ADOS Algorithm Cutoff	
		Autism Spectrum	Autism
Communication	4	2	3
Reciprocal social interaction	6	4	6
Stereotyped behaviors and restricted interests	0	No cutoffs determined	
Imagination/creativity	2	No cutoffs determined	
Communication and social interaction total	10	7	10

of a particular type is likely to occur. Across the session the examiner presents numerous opportunities for the individual being assessed to exhibit behaviors of interest in the diagnostic process. A module chosen to be appropriate to a particular developmental and language level dictates the protocol. At the end of the administration, ratings are completed based on the observation period. The obtained scores are compared with the ADOS cutoff scores to assist in diagnosis. Scores at or above the cutoff indicate a higher likelihood of an ASD.

For this assessment as well, all of the required items from module 4 were administered. Module 4 is appropriate for an adolescent or an adult who has fluent speech. The descriptions provided below involve only those behaviors and clinical impressions that are needed to ascertain the presence of autistic traits.

Language and Communication: Sam's overall level of language was appropriate, but he often spoke in a very monotone and flat voice. Sam did not display any immediate or delayed echolalia during our time together and did not use any stereotyped or idiosyncratic words or phrases. While Sam would spontaneously offer information about his thoughts, feeling, and experiences, he would do so in an excessive, almost-rambling manner in which he provided too much information. Sam would only occasionally ask the examiner about his own thoughts and had difficulty sustaining a reciprocal conversation. Sam did display some descriptive gestures during the ADOS, but they were rather limited in range, and he did not display any empathic or emotional gestures.

Reciprocal Social Interaction: Sam's eye contact during our time together was somewhat appropriate but not always. He would occasionally direct some facial expressions toward the examiner but less so than would be expected. Sam displayed some interest in the examiner and communicated some degree of understanding of others' emotions. While Sam was able to provide the examiner with several examples of insight and some examples of personal responsibility, they were less so than would be expected from someone his age. Sam's social overtures were slightly unusual, as they would often relate to his own interests, and only minimal attempts were made to include the examiner. While a good rapport was developed between Sam and the examiner, there was minimal reciprocal communication. Although Sam was very verbal throughout our time together, the vast majority of Sam's speech consisted of asking for clarification from the examiner because of his high level of anxiety.

Stereotyped Behaviors/Restricted Interests: Sam did not display any unusual sensory interest or hand or finger mannerism. He did not engage in any self-injurious behaviors, excessive interests in specific topics, or any compulsions or rituals.

Imagination/Creativity: Sam displayed a great deal of difficulty in the areas of the ADOS that required creative or make-believe actions. During the "Create A Story" section, Sam displayed tremendous difficulty coming up with an imaginative story using a few random objects and his creativity.

Other Abnormal Behaviors: Sam displayed some anxiety throughout the assessment, but it did not become extreme enough to cause problems during our time together.

Vineland Adaptive Behavior Scales (Parents as Respondent)[1]

Domain	Standard Score	Adaptive Level	Age Equivalent
Communication Domain	25	Low	
Receptive		Low	2 years 10 months
Expressive		Low	8 years 0 months
Written		Moderately low	12 years 0 months
Daily Living Skills Domain	65	Low	
Personal		Moderately low	16 years 0 months
Domestic		Low	12 years 0 months
Community		Low	15 years 9 months
Socialization Domain	30	Low	
Interpersonal relationships		Low	2 years 10 months
Play and leisure time		Low	5 years 4 months
Coping skills		Low	8 years 6 months
Adaptive Behavior Composite	38	Low	

The information provided by Sam's parents finds him to be functioning below one tenth of the first percentile of people his age in the realms of communication and socialization. Sam was at the first percentile of people his age in the realm

[1] *Vineland Adaptive Behavior Scales, Second Edition (Vineland-II).* Copyright © 2005 NCS Pearson, Inc. Reproduced with permission. All rights reserved.

of daily living skills. In terms of Sam's communication skills, he is probably functioning at an elementary school level. In regard to socialization, Sam is probably functioning at the kindergarten or first-grade level. If left to his own devices, Sam would not make any attempts to socialize with others and would spend the majority of his time alone, in his room.

Treatment Plan

Sam clearly meets and exceeds all of the diagnostic criteria for having autism according to *DSM-IV-TR* code 299.00. Sam has a lifelong history of difficulty because of his autism. He is now in significant need of Regional Center services to help him develop the occupational and life skills he requires to become a functioning member of society.

Sam is in need of job coaching to assist him in finding an appropriate vocation in which his autism and high level of anxiety will not become detriments to his success. Sam also requires life skills training to help prepare him to be able to live independently. The parents noted that Sam does not have the basic skills necessary to be financially independent.

References

American Psychiatric Association. (1987). *Diagnostic and Statistical Manual of Mental Disorders* (3rd ed., rev.). Washington, DC: Author.

American Psychiatric Association. (1994). *Diagnostic and Statistical Manual of Mental Disorders* (4th ed.). Washington, DC: Author.

American Psychiatric Association. (2000). *Diagnostic and Statistical Manual of Mental Disorders* (4th ed., rev.). Washington, DC: Author.

Capone, G. T. (2001). "Down syndrome and autistic spectrum disorder: A look at what we know." *Down's Syndrome Association Journal* 97, pp. 6–13.

Exner, J. E. & Weiner, I. B. (1994). *The Rorschach: A Comprehensive System Volume 3: Assessment of Children and Adolescents* (2nd ed.). New York: Wiley.

Happe, F. G. (1995). "The role of age and verbal ability in the theory of mind task performance of subjects with autism." *Child Development* 66(3), pp. 843–855.

Houston, R. & Frith, U. (2000). *Autism in History: The Case of Hugh Blair of Borgue.* Oxford, UK: Blackwell.

Kanner, L. (1943) "Autistic disturbances of affective contact." *Nervous Child* 2, pp. 217–250.

Kennedy, D., Banks, R., & Grandin, T. (2002). *The ADHD-Autism Connection: A Step toward More Accurate Diagnoses and Effective Treatments.* Colorado Springs, Colorado: Waterbrook Press.

Klin, A., Jones, W., Schultz, R., Volkmar, F., & Cohen, D. (2002). "Visual fixation patterns during viewing of naturalistic social situations as predictors of social competence in individuals with autism." *Archives of General Psychiatry*, 59, pp. 809–816.

Vatter, G. (1998). "Diagnosis of autism in children with Down syndrome." Retrieved from http://www.altonweb.com/cs/downsyndrome/index.htm?page=autism.html. (accessed September 2009).

Wechsler, D. (2003). *WISC-IV Administration and Scoring Manual.* San Antonio, Texas: The Psychological Corporation.

Wing, L. (1981). "Asperger syndrome: A clinical account." *Psychological Medicine*, 11, pp. 115–130.

http://www.ed.gov/about/offices/list/ocr/504faq.html (accessed September, 2009).

http://en.wikipedia.org/wiki/Agenesis_of_the_corpus_callosum (accessed September, 2009).

Index

ADHD *see* attention-deficit/hyperactivity disorder
ADI-R *see* Autism Diagnostic Interview–Revised
ADOS *see* Autism Diagnostic Observation Schedule
adult patients 12, 14, 16, 18, 27–8, 29–30, 35, 46, 85,
    97–104, 120–1, 130–1, 133–5, 149,
    169–78
agenesis of the corpus callosum 35–6
ages at diagnosis 16, 18, 21, 50, 52–3, 87–95, 97–104,
    106, 147–8
anxiety disorder 127, 172–8
APGAR scores 35
appendices 151–78
ASDs *see* autism spectrum disorders
Asperger, Hans 2
Asperger's disorder 2, 6, 14, 39, 40–1, 45–6,
    61–3, 97–8, 100, 103–4, 117, 118–21, 124–5, 128,
    134, 140, 146, 148–9, 171 autism
    118–21
    concepts 2, 14, 39, 40–1, 45–6, 61–3, 97–8, 100,
    103–4, 117, 118–21, 124–5, 128, 134, 140, 146,
    148–9, 171
    DSM-IV-TR criteria 39, 40–1, 45–6, 61–3
    IQ levels 120, 148, 171
    symptoms 39, 40–1, 45, 61 3, 97–8, 100, 103–4,
    117, 118–21, 124–5, 171
assessment devices
    see also Autism Diagnostic...; screening tools
    concepts 25–9, 49, 55, 143–5, 157, 161, 164, 165–9,
    172–8
assessments 2–3, 5, 12–15, 17–31, 46–60, 61–77,
    132–3, 143–9, 151–6, 157–78
    see also evaluations
assistance from schools 148–9, 160–1, 169
attending parties
    evaluations 13–15, 17–18, 82–3, 143–4, 145–6
    feedback issues 145–6
attention-deficit/hyperactivity disorder (ADHD) 35,
    54, 57, 89, 108–9, 122–7, 142, 164–5
atypical autism 39
    see also pervasive developmental disorder...

author's questionnaire 151–6
autism 1–3, 5–16, 28–9, 39–43, 46–60, 61–77, 79–85,
    105, 117–49, 157–78
    see also causes...; diagnosis; evaluations; questions;
    referrals; treatments
    ADHD 122–7, 142
    Asperger's disorder 118–21
    comorbidities 117–42, 145
    definitions 1–2
    depression 11, 127, 136–7, 145–6, 172–8
    differential diagnosis through the lifespan 117–42
    Down's syndrome 131–3
    DSM-IV-TR criteria 2, 28–9, 39–43, 46–60, 61–77,
    79–85, 105, 117–18, 121–8, 172, 178
    expressive language delay 127, 137–8, 142, 153–4,
    158–61, 162–3, 177–8
    Fragile X syndrome 131–2
    high-functioning autism 117–18, 119–22, 128–9,
    140–1, 146, 147–8
    historical background 1–3
    management 3, 21–2, 118, 125, 147–9, 160–1, 163,
    169, 178
    mental retardation 28, 127–31, 145, 148–9
    obsessive-compulsive disorder 80, 83–4, 114, 127,
    141–2
    oppositional defiant disorder 127, 138–40
    prevalence 2, 128, 133, 134
    prognosis 147–9
    remitting disorder aspects 47, 48, 87–9
    schizoid personality disorder 41, 133–5
    selective mutism 140–1
    social phobia 52–7, 135–6
    symptoms 1–2, 7–9, 12–13, 15, 16, 18, 20, 24–6,
    30–1, 36, 37–8, 39–43, 46–60, 61–77, 79–85,
    105–15, 117–27, 146–7, 157–78
Autism and Developmental Disabilities Monitoring
    Network (ADDM Network) 2
Autism Diagnostic Interview–Revised (ADI-R)
    benefits 26–7
    concepts 25–9, 49, 143, 157, 164, 166–9, 172–5

Autism Diagnostic Observation Schedule (ADOS)
    benefits 25–6, 55
    concepts 25–9, 49, 55, 67, 124–5, 143, 157, 161, 164,
        166–9, 172, 175–8
autism spectrum disorders (ASDs)
    see also autism
    ADHD 122–7, 142
    concepts 2–3, 5–16, 28–9, 39–43, 46–60, 61–77,
        79–85, 105, 114, 117–49, 157–78
    differential diagnosis through the lifespan
        117–42
    DSM-IV-TR criteria 2, 28–9, 39–43, 46–60, 61–77,
        79–85, 105, 117–18, 121–8, 172, 178
    management 3, 21–2, 118, 125, 147–9, 160–1, 163,
        169, 178
    prevalence 2, 128, 133, 134
avoidant personality disorder, concepts 41–2, 97–8

babies
    overly easy babies 107
    pregnancy history 35–6, 152, 158–9, 162, 165, 172
    separation anxiety 106
Bassett, Sue 19, 25–6, 160–1
Bayley Scales of Infant Development–Second Edition
    assessment 145
behaviors 15, 19, 20, 39–43, 45–60, 79–85, 87–8, 93–5,
        105–15, 117–18, 120–7, 130–1, 134–7, 146–9,
        154–78
    see also intense focus; motor...; nonverbal...;
        repetitive...; rituals; routines
    adult interview questions 101–4
    concepts 40–3, 79–85, 87–8, 93–5, 115, 117–18,
        120–7, 130–1, 134–7, 146–9, 154–6
    DSM-IV-TR criteria 39–43, 79–85
bipolar disorder 45
    see also depression
body language 39–41, 46–52, 88, 101–2, 123–4, 138–9,
        144, 163, 173
body postures 39–41, 46–52, 88, 123–4, 153,
        175–8
boys
    speech development 8, 37
    toilet training 38, 152, 159, 162, 165, 172
brain injuries 63
bright lights 111–21, 155–6

California's Department of Developmental Disorders
    28
Capone, George T. 133
car accidents 36
case coordinators 19–20
causes of autism 35–6, 131–3
Centers for Disease Control and Prevention (CDC) 2,
    128
Childhood Disintegrative Disorder, DSM-IV-TR
    criteria 39, 40
chromosomal/genetic problems 36, 131–3
classification methods
    see also Autism Diagnostic...; screening tools
    concepts 26–7
clothes, sensory integration issues 111–12,
    155–6

cognitive assessments, concepts 27–9
communications 5–6, 7–8, 10, 12–13, 21, 26, 30–1,
        36, 37–8, 40–3, 59–60, 61–77, 87–8, 91–3,
        100–2, 117–18, 119–27, 130–1, 134–8,
        152–78
    see also language...; speech...
comorbidities 117–42, 145
conclusions, diagnosis 143–9
concrete use of language, concepts 70–2, 154
conduct of evaluations 17–31, 145–9
conversational impairment problems
    see also language...
    concepts 40–3, 63–6, 74, 91–3, 100–2, 119–21,
        124–7, 153–4, 167–78
corpus callosum 35–6
Cub Scouts 57
cuddles 105–6, 155–6, 159, 163, 174–8
    see also physical affection
cultural issues, parent/patient agreement with the
        diagnosis 14–16, 18

dating 99–100
day care providers 13
daydreaming 127
delivery considerations, diagnosis 16
depression, concepts 11, 45, 127, 136–7, 145–6, 172–8
detached personality disorders 41–2, 133–5
    see also avoidant...; schizoid...
developmental milestones 8, 37–8, 40–1, 62–3, 74–7,
        87–8, 135–6, 154, 159, 162–3, 165, 172
diagnosis
    ages at diagnosis 16, 18, 21, 50, 52–3, 87–95,
        97–104, 106, 147–8
    Asperger's disorder 39, 40–1, 45, 61–3, 97–8, 100,
        103–4, 117, 124–5, 146, 148–9
    concepts 2–3, 5, 9–13, 14–16, 21, 39–43, 105–15,
        117–42, 157–78
    conclusions 143–9
    DSM-IV-TR criteria 2, 28–9, 39–43, 45–60, 61–77,
        79–85, 105, 117–18, 121–8, 172, 178
    non-DSM-IV symptoms 105–15
    PDD-NOS 39, 41–2, 61–2, 67, 117, 121–2, 165
    responses 15–16, 146–9
    timescales 27, 30–1
Diagnostic and Statistical Manual of Mental Disorders,
        Fourth Edition (DSM-IV)
    Asperger's disorder criteria 39, 40–1, 45–6, 61–3
    autistic disorder criteria 2, 28–9, 39–43, 46–60,
        61–77, 79–85, 105, 117–18, 121–8,
        172, 178
    PDD-NOS criteria 39, 41–2, 121–2, 133–4
DNA screen 36
Down's syndrome (trisomy 21), concepts 131–3
DSM-IIIR *see Diagnostic and Statistical Manual of*
        Mental Disorders, Third Edition–Revised
DSM-IV... *see Diagnostic and Statistical Manual of*
        Mental Disorders, Fourth Edition

echolalia, concepts 67–8, 136, 154, 176–8
education
    parents 148–9, 160–1
    professionals 3, 5, 15, 22–3

elementary schools 8, 18, 29, 34–5, 50–4, 55–7, 64–5, 71–2, 88, 89–91, 92, 94–5, 101, 135–6, 148–9, 170–2
  see also schools
emotional reciprocity problems *see* reciprocity problems
empathy 2, 97–8, 103–4
employers 18, 35, 97–104, 120–1, 130–1, 134–5, 169, 170–1, 178
encompassing preoccupations
  see also intense focus on objects
  concepts 37, 40–1, 52, 64, 72–4, 79–85, 93–5, 101, 104, 119–21, 125–6, 134–6, 154–5, 166–9, 173–8
evaluations 2–3, 5, 7–15, 17–31, 33–8, 46–60, 61–77, 87–95, 97–104, 121–2, 125, 132–3, 136–7, 143–9, 151–6, 157–78
  see also assessments; Autism Diagnostic...; screening...
evaluators, previous evaluations 9–11
expressive language delay
  see also talking ages
  concepts 127, 137–8, 142, 153–4, 158–61, 162–3, 177–8
eye contact 10, 13, 14, 20, 24, 26, 33, 39–43, 46–52, 87–8, 98–9, 100, 106, 123–7, 138–9, 143–4, 153, 155–6, 159–61, 162–3, 166–9, 172–8
  see also social impairment problems

facial expressions 39–41, 46–52, 88, 123–4
fathers 13–14, 23, 94, 147–9
  see also parents
feedback issues
  attending parties 145–6
  concepts 143–9
financial consequences of diagnosis 10–11
flapping hands 15, 19, 20, 30, 40, 81, 83–4, 129–31, 134–5, 138, 143–4, 149, 154–5
  see also motor...; repetitive behavior...
'flipping' pronouns, concepts 67, 136, 154, 167–9
fluorescent lights 111–12
food, picky eaters 109–11, 134–5, 148, 155–6, 160
Fragile X syndrome 36, 131–3
Frith, Uta 59

GARS *see* Gilliam Autism Rating Scale
Gesell assessment 145
gestures 39–43, 62–3, 88, 123–4, 152–6
Gilliam Autism Rating Scale (GARS), concepts 23, 25
girls
  speech development 8, 37
  toilet training 38, 152
gut feelings/instincts, diagnosis 144

handshakes 24
head-banging behaviors
  see also motor problems
  concepts 83–4, 149, 157–61
hearing 36, 37, 47–8, 152–3, 164–5
high-functioning autism, concepts 117–18, 119–22, 128–9, 140–1, 146, 147–8
historical background of autism 1–3

historical information requirements, evaluations 13–14, 18, 19–22, 26, 29–30, 33–8, 47, 87–95, 97–104, 121–2, 136–7, 143–4, 146–7, 151–6, 158–9, 161–3, 164–6, 170–2
hugging 105–6, 155–6, 160, 163, 174–8
  see also physical affection

idiosyncratic language
  see also language impairment problems
  concepts 40–3, 66–74, 119–21, 134–5, 154, 176–8
  definition 66
IEPs *see* Individualized Educational Plans
imaginative play 26, 30, 39–40, 46–7, 52–9, 74–7, 80, 87–8, 119–21, 130, 135–6, 138, 154, 155–6, 166–9, 173–8
  see also play
  concepts 40–3, 74–7, 80, 87–8, 138, 154, 155–6
imitation of others, non-DSM-IV symptoms 113, 156, 158–61, 175
in-denial parents 7, 11–12, 14–15, 20–1, 36, 147
inappropriate behaviors 51–2, 72, 112–13
Individualized Educational Plans (IEPs), concepts 8–9, 34–5, 120–1, 148–9, 162–3, 165
inflexible adherence to routines/rituals
  see also behaviors; rituals; routines
  concepts 40–1, 81–3, 99–100, 102–3, 126–7, 134–5, 137, 139–40, 154–5, 160–1, 167–9, 173–8
information requirements, evaluations 13–14, 18, 19–22, 26, 29–30, 33–8, 47, 87–95, 97–104, 121–2, 136–7, 143–4, 146–7, 151–6, 158–9, 164–6, 170–2
instincts, diagnosis 144
institutions, fears of consequences of diagnosis 18
intense focus on objects 37, 40–1, 52, 64, 72–4, 79–85, 92, 93–5, 101–2, 104, 120–1, 125–6, 137, 154–5, 166–9, 173–8
  see also behaviors
interviews
  see also questions
  ADI-R 25–9, 49, 143, 157, 164, 166–9, 172–5
  author's questionnaire 151–6
  conduct of evaluations 17–31, 145–9
  feedback issues 143–9
  uses 22–3, 66
IQ tests 27–9, 45, 120, 127–31, 143, 165, 171
  see also Stanford–Binet...; WAIS...; WISC...

Kaiser-Permanente 5–6, 15, 19, 100, 131–2, 160–1
Kanner, Leo 1–2
Kennedy, Diane 122–3
kindergarten 47, 49–52, 54–5, 56–7, 66, 69, 88, 89–91, 94–5, 101, 114, 118, 124, 135–7, 164–5
  see also preschool children; schools
Kohlberg's stages of moral development 70

lack of fear, non-DSM-IV symptoms 108–9
language impairment problems 5–8, 10–13, 21, 26, 30–1, 36, 37–8, 40–3, 59–60, 61–77, 87–8, 91–3, 100–2, 117–18, 119–27, 130–1, 134–41, 145, 146–9, 152–78
  see also conversational...; hearing...; idiosyncratic...; speech...; stereotyped...

language impairment problems (*Cont'd.*)
  adult interview questions 100–2
  author's questionnaire 153–4
  concepts 40–3, 61–77, 87–8, 91–3, 100–2, 117–18,
    119–21, 130–1, 134–41, 146–9, 152–6, 158–61
  DSM-IV-TR ... 40–3, 61, 117, 121–3
  expressive language delay 127, 137–8, 142, 153–4,
    158–61, 162–3, 177–8
  mental retardation 130–1
  questions 61–77, 87–8, 91–3, 100–2, 153–6
  receptive language delay 21, 28–9, 36, 40–3, 61,
    62–3, 117–18, 119–22, 130–1, 136, 137–8, 152–4,
    158–61, 164–5, 170–1, 177–8
  selective mutism 140–1
  talking ages 33, 37–8, 61–3, 117–18, 121–2, 131,
    134, 136, 142, 162, 165
  teenager interview questions 87–8, 91–3
Leslie, Alan 59
life skills 178
lights 111–21, 155–6
lines from movies, concepts 68–70, 154
lining-up toys, non-DSM-IV symptoms 113–14, 130,
    141–2, 155–6, 160
literal/concrete use of language
  see also language impairment problems
  concepts 70–2, 154
'the little professor syndrome' 63–4, 72–4, 79, 101–2,
    119–21, 154, 173–4
loud noises, sensory integration issues 21–2, 112,
    155–6, 174–8

management of ASDs
  assistance from schools 148–9, 160–1, 169
  concepts 3, 21–2, 118, 125, 147–9, 160–1, 163, 169,
    178
marriage 49, 99–100, 134
medical problems with patients 35–6, 38, 49–50, 63,
    152–3, 158–60, 162–3, 165, 172
mental health professionals, sources of referrals 5–6,
    15, 24, 33–4, 137–8
mental retardation 28, 127–31, 145, 148–9
middle-of-a-thought talking
  see also theory of mind
  concepts 92–3
mime, speech delays 40–3, 62–3, 138, 153–4
misdiagnosis problems 2–3, 7–8, 9–11, 13, 15, 20,
    22–3, 45–6, 134, 144–5
Modified Checklist for Autism in Toddlers 23
modulation aspects of eye contact 48–9, 106
mothers 5, 12–14, 18, 21, 23, 35–6, 65–6, 75–7, 89–95,
    101–4, 110–14, 132–3, 136–7, 147–9, 157–78
  see also parents
motor problems
  see also behaviors; repetitive...
  concepts 15, 19, 20, 21–2, 30, 37–8, 40–3, 81, 83–4,
    112–13, 129–31, 134–5, 137, 143–4, 148–9,
    152–6, 157–61, 162–3, 173–8

neurologists 5–6, 8, 18, 19, 21, 35–6
neurotypical, definition 93
noises 21–2, 112, 155–6, 174–8
nonverbal behaviors

  see also eye contact; social impairment problems
  concepts 39–41, 45–52, 88, 99–102,
    123–7, 138–9, 153, 159–61, 162–3, 166–9,
    172–8
  DSM-IV-TR criteria 39–41, 46–52

observations 5, 19–22, 25–30, 49, 52–4, 55, 67, 124–5,
    143, 145, 156, 157, 161, 162–3, 164, 166–9, 172,
    175–8
obsessive-compulsive disorder (OCD)
  autism 141–2
  concepts 80, 83–4, 114, 127, 141–2
  DSM-IV-TR criteria 142
occupational therapists 8, 19, 21–2, 34–5, 158,
    163, 178
occupational therapy/sensory integration evaluations
  (OT/3Is), concepts 21–2
OCD *see* obsessive-compulsive disorder
ODD *see* oppositional defiant disorder
office evaluations, critique 29–30
oppositional defiant disorder (ODD), concepts 127,
    138–40
'out of sight, out of mind' philosophy 55–6
overly easy babies 107

pain tolerance, non-DSM-IV symptoms 113, 156
parents 5–7, 9, 11–18, 19–22, 23, 26, 29–31, 33–6,
    46–8, 65–77, 89–95, 101–4, 110–14, 132–3,
    136–9, 143–9, 157–78
  see also fathers; mothers
  agreement with the diagnosis 6–7, 11–13, 14–16, 49,
    125–6, 147–9
  attending parties 13–15, 17–18, 143–4, 145–6
  education needs 148–9, 160–1
  feedback 143–9
  historical information requirements 13–14, 18,
    19–22, 26, 29–30, 33–8, 47, 87–95, 121–2,
    136–7, 143–4, 146–7, 151–6, 158–9, 161–3,
    164–6, 170–2
  in-denial types 7, 11–12, 14–15, 20–1, 36, 147
  pre-formed opinions 7
  privacy concerns 17–18, 21
  questionnaires 23–5, 151–6
  referrals 5, 6–9, 12–13, 33–4, 169
  responses to the diagnosis 15–16, 146–9
  reticent parents 6–7, 14–16, 20–1, 36, 147
  rewriting of history 12–13, 20–1
  sources of referrals 5–7, 9, 12–13, 33–4, 169
Parrish, Jerrold 125
patients
  see also adult...; autism; teenagers
  agreement with the diagnosis 11–13, 14–16, 49,
    125–6, 147–9
  conduct of evaluations 17–31, 145–9
  feedback 143–9
  medical problems 35–6, 38, 49–50, 63, 152–3,
    158–60, 162–3, 165, 172
  responses to the diagnosis 15–16, 146–9
PDD-NOS *see* pervasive developmental disorder – Not
  Otherwise Specified
pediatricians 5–6, 7–8, 10, 18, 19–21, 24, 35–6, 82–3,
    137–8

peer relationships 20–1, 26–7, 39–42, 45–6, 52–7,
    88–90, 97–100, 103–4, 121–7, 130–3, 135–41,
    153–78
  see also social impairment problems
persistent preoccupation with parts of objects
  see also behaviors
  concepts 40–1, 84–5, 115, 130–1, 137,
    154–5
personal space 51–2, 173
pervasive developmental disorder – Not Otherwise
    Specified (PDD-NOS)
  concepts 2, 39, 41–2, 43, 61–2, 67, 117, 121–2,
    133–4, 165, 175–6
  DSM-IV-TR criteria 39, 41–2, 121–2, 133–4
physical affection
  see also cuddles; hugging
  non-DSM-IV symptoms 105–6, 155–6
picky eaters, non-DSM-IV symptoms 109–11, 134–5,
    148, 155–6, 160
play 26, 30, 39–40, 46–7, 52–9, 74–7, 80, 87–8, 107–8,
    119–21, 130, 135–6, 138, 154, 155–6, 159–60,
    162–3, 166–9, 173–8
  see also imaginative...
  concepts 40–3, 56–7, 74–7, 80, 87–8, 107–8, 119–21,
    135–6, 138, 154, 155–6, 162–3
  developmental milestones 74–5, 87–8, 135–6, 154,
    165
play dates 55–7, 138
playgrounds 53–4
pragmatics
  see also conversational impairment problems
  concepts 64–6, 91–3, 101–2, 118, 149
pre-formed opinions of parents 7
pregnancy history 35–6, 152, 158–9, 162, 165, 172
preschool children 8, 18, 29, 34–5, 47, 49–53, 54,
    56–7
  see also kindergarten
previous evaluations 7–13, 24, 34–6, 122–3,
    126–7
privacy concerns of parents 17–18, 21
professionals
  critique 21–2, 126–7
  education needs 3, 5, 15, 18–31
  previous evaluations 7–13, 24, 34–6, 122–3, 126–7
  sources of referrals 5–6, 7–8, 15, 24, 33–4, 137–8
  types 5–6, 7–8, 10, 18, 19, 21
prognosis, autism 147–9
pronomal reversal, concepts 67
psychiatrists 8, 10, 18, 19, 21, 22
psychological tests 5, 22–3, 28, 34–5, 45–6
psychologist 8, 10, 28
psychotic disorders 1, 29, 41, 43, 122, 145
  see also schizophrenia

quantitative instruments, critique 22–3, 26
questionnaires
  see also Childhood Autism...; Gilliam Autism...;
    screening...
  concepts 23–5, 151–6
questions 5, 6, 9–10, 17–18, 21–2, 23–5, 33–8, 66–77,
    80–5, 87–95, 97–104, 143–9, 151–6
  see also interviews

receptive language delay 21, 28–9, 36, 40–3, 61, 62–3,
    117–18, 119–22, 130–1, 136, 137–8, 152–4,
    158–61, 164–5, 170–1, 177–8
reciprocity problems
  see also social impairment...
  concepts 39–43, 59–60, 92–3, 153
reevaluations, very young children 144–5, 163
references 179–80
referrals
  concepts 5–16, 24, 30–1, 33–4, 137–8, 143–9, 169
  feedback issues 143–9
Regional Centers 8, 11, 31, 34–5, 67, 145, 148–9,
    160–1, 164–5, 169, 178
remitting disorder aspects of autism 47, 48, 87–9
repeating/reciting lines from movies, concepts 68–70,
    154
repetitive behavior/interests/activities 15, 19, 20,
    40–3, 46, 79–85, 87–8, 93–5, 126, 129–31, 134,
    137–8, 154–6, 157–61, 162–3, 166–9, 173–8
  see also behaviors
repetitive motor problems 15, 19, 20, 30, 40–3, 81,
    83–4, 129–31, 134–5, 137–8, 143–4, 148–9,
    152–6, 157–61, 162–3, 173–8
repetitive use of language
  see also language impairment problems
  concepts 66–74, 119–21, 154
report cards 35
responses to the diagnosis 15–16, 146–9
reticent parents 6–7, 14–16, 20–1, 36, 147
Rett's disorder, DSM-IV-TR criteria 39, 40
rewriting of history, parents 12–13, 20–1
rituals
  see also behaviors
  concepts 40–3, 56–7, 81–3, 99–100, 102–3, 126–7,
    134–5, 137, 139–40, 154–5, 167–9, 173–8
robotic/monotone voices, concepts 72, 154, 172, 176–8
Rorschach inkblot test 29
routines
  see also behaviors
  concepts 40–3, 56–7, 81–3, 99–100, 102–3, 126–7,
    134–5, 137, 139–40, 154–5, 160–1, 167–9,
    173–8
rules 56–7, 90

sample copies of reports 157–78
Sam's report, sample copies of reports 169–78
sarcasm 71–2
schizoid personality disorder
  concepts 41, 133–5
  DSM-IV-TR criteria 133
schizophrenia 1, 29, 41, 43, 122
  see also psychotic disorders
schools 8–9, 18, 29, 34–5, 47, 49–54, 55–7, 64–5, 71–2,
    88–91, 92, 94–5, 101, 135–7, 144–5, 148–9,
    170–2
screening teams
  see also teams
  concepts 19–25
screening tools
  see also assessment devices; Childhood Autism...;
    Gilliam Autism...; IQ...; questionnaires
  author's questionnaire 151–6

screening tools (*Cont'd.*)
  concepts 22–5, 128–30, 143–5, 151–6, 157, 161, 164,
    165–9, 172–8
  critique 23
  types 23, 25, 128–30, 143, 151–6
second opinions 24
Section 504 plans 34–5
selective mutism, concepts 140–1
self-stim behaviors
  see also motor problems
  concepts 83–4, 114–15
sensory integration issues, non-DSM-IV symptoms
    111–13, 114–15, 134–5, 148–9, 155–6, 160,
    167–9, 174–8
separation anxiety, non-DSM-IV symptoms 106, 108
service providers 34–5
sex 45, 72, 91–3, 99–100
shared enjoyment/interests/achievements with others
  see also social impairment problems
  concepts 39–43, 57–9, 90–1, 163, 166–9
showing/bringing/pointing-out objects of interest,
    concepts 39–43, 51–2, 57–9, 90–1, 153, 159–60,
    163, 166–9
shyness 52–7, 135–6
'slow-to-warm' children 52–3
social impairment problems 1–2, 6–13, 18, 20, 24, 26,
    28–9, 30–1, 35, 39–43, 45–60, 87–91, 97–100,
    105–15, 117–18, 120–38, 140–2, 145, 146–9,
    153–78
  see also nonverbal...; peer...; reciprocity...; shared
    enjoyment...
  adult interview questions 85, 97–100
  author's questionnaire 153
  concepts 39–43, 45–60, 87–91, 97–100, 117–18,
    120–38, 140–2, 146–9, 153–6
  DSM-IV-TR criteria 39–43, 46–60, 121–7
  mental retardation 129–30
  questions 46–60, 87–91, 97–100
  schizoid personality disorder 133–5
  teenager interview questions 87–91, 136–7
social phobia
  concepts 52–7, 135–6
  DSM-IV-TR criteria 135
speech delays 21, 28–9, 30–1, 40–3, 61, 62–3, 117–18,
    119–22, 130–1, 136, 137–8, 153–4, 158–61,
    162–3, 177–8
speech therapists 5–6, 7–8, 10, 21, 31, 137–8, 145, 163,
    165
  see also language impairment problems
Stanford–Binet IQ test 128–9
stereotyped behavior/interests/activities 15, 19, 20,
    40–3, 46, 79–85, 87–8, 93–5, 126, 134–6, 154–6,
    159–61, 162–3, 166–9, 173–8
  see also behaviors
stereotyped use of language
  see also language impairment problems
  concepts 40–3, 66–74, 119–21, 154–6, 175–8
  definition 66
stranger danger, non-DSM-IV symptoms 108–9
Sullivan, Kathy 144

Sushinsky, Len 100
symptoms
  see also behaviors; language...; social...
  ADHD 35, 54, 57, 89, 108–9, 122–7, 142
  Asperger's disorder 39, 40–1, 45, 61–3, 97–8, 100,
    103–4, 117, 118–21, 124–5, 171
  autism 1–3, 7–9, 12–13, 15, 16, 18, 20, 24–6, 30–1,
    36, 37–8, 39–43, 46–60, 61–77, 79–85, 105–15,
    117–27, 146–7, 157–78
  DSM-IV-TR criteria 2, 28–9, 39–43, 46–60, 61–77,
    79–85, 105, 117–18, 121–7
  non-DSM-IV symptoms 105–15
  PDD-NOS 39, 41–2, 61–2, 67, 117, 121–2, 133–4,
    165

'tag teams' 19–20
talking ages 33, 37–8, 61–3, 117–18, 121–2, 131, 134,
    136, 142, 162, 165
  see also expressive language...; language...
teachers 13, 18, 34–5, 82–3, 137–8, 144–5, 164–5
team sports 57
teams
  see also screening...
  concepts 19–25
teenagers 14, 16, 18, 26, 29–30, 46, 85, 87–95, 130–1,
    136–9, 145, 149, 163–9
temper tantrums 81–3, 139
'tests' 5, 22–3, 27–9, 34–5, 45–6, 120, 127–31,
    143–4
  see also Childhood Autism...; Gilliam Autism...
theory of mind
  see also middle-of-a-thought talking; reciprocity
    problems
  concepts 59–60, 92–3
third-party information, evaluations 13–15, 17–18,
    21–2, 34–5, 82–3, 143, 144–5
Thomas the Train character 80–1, 94–5, 118, 120, 141
timescales, evaluations 27, 30–1
toilet training 37, 38, 152, 159, 162, 165, 172
toys 13, 17, 19–20, 26, 80–1, 84–5, 90–1, 103–4,
    113–14, 118, 130, 138, 141–2, 155–6, 159–61,
    162–3
'trashcan diagnosis' 87
treatments 21–2, 118, 125, 148–9, 160–1, 163, 169, 178
  see also management...
trisomy 21 *see* Down's syndrome (trisomy 21)

Vineland-II 27, 143, 145, 165, 169, 172
visual stims, non-DSM-IV symptoms 114–15

WAIS-III IQ test 27, 128–9
wandering away, non-DSM-IV symptoms 107–8, 125,
    155–6, 160, 163
waving goodbye 106
Wechsler tests *see* WAIS...; WISC...
WISC-IV IQ test 27, 128–9

'zoning out', evaluations 125–6, 142

Index compiled by Terry Halliday